What's the Matter?

The Story of Atoms and Molecules

Sunnie Kim and Lisa Melton
Illustrated by Dirk Wunderlich and Phil Ortiz

Copyright ©1999 by Science-Kids Publishing, Inc.
All rights reserved. Activity pages intended for
students to use in classrooms may be duplicated.
All other text may not be reproduced in any form
or by any means without the publisher's
permission. For further information, please contact
Science-Kids Publishing, Inc.
www.science-kids.com

ISBN: 1-891418-14-9

Contributing Writers: Sunnie Kim, Lisa Melton, & Dennis Lamour
Contributing Artists: Dirk Wunderlich & Phil Ortiz

Manufactured in the United States of America

Note to Parents and Teachers

Science is an integral part of our everyday lives. More so now than ever before in our history, it is critical that children grasp scientific concepts so they may succeed in the challenges of the future. The **SCIENCE-KIDS LEARNING ACTIVITY BOOK** series builds scientific literacy through a systematic presentation of the National Academy of Sciences' **National Science Education Content Standards**.

The first title in the series, *What's the Matter?*, introduces readers to the world of atoms and molecules—the very foundation of chemistry and physics. The lively and humorous text is sure to entice youngsters into this world, and once there, they'll be fascinated! Some of the scientific concepts covered are:

⇨ the definition of matter
⇨ atoms, elements, and ions
⇨ atomic bonding and molecules
⇨ the properties of atoms and molecules
⇨ the Periodic Table of the Elements
⇨ the Atomic Shell Model

How to Use This Book

What's the Matter? presents a wonderful opportunity for young readers to learn about chemistry. The book is divided into different sections, as indicated by each new headline. Tell your child or students to pay attention to the words printed in bold. These are new science terms for that section. By the end of each section,

> **For Teachers:** Read each section together as a class. Encourage questions about concepts or words that aren't clear to your students. Once the class reading is completed, students can work independently on the activities in that section.

> **Group Projects:** Some of the activities in *What's the Matter?* may be expanded for group projects in the classroom. These are identified with a **C**. Please review in advance the group activities to be sure all the materials needed are on hand for your students to use. You can split up the students into groups. Encourage the kids to talk about the activity, question each other, and especially to draw pictures of what they've learned. Modeling the scientific ideas on paper will go a long way toward understanding each lesson.

readers can "Check Out the Science Words!"—a list of the new vocabulary words they've encountered. In checking off each word, children can monitor their progress on mastering concepts.

Throughout the book, children will also find interesting, skill-building activities that aid in learning science—and especially in having fun. The activities, and experiments, too, are designed to reinforce the scientific concepts your child or students are learning; they'll also encourage children to explore science in everyday life. The answers to the exercises can be found near the end of this book.

Last, but definitely not least, a certificate of completion awaits your child or student on the last page of *What's the Matter?* When the book has been completed, reward your young reader with this honor. Children develop a sense of academic achievement when their efforts at learning are valued and appreciated. The recognition will also give your child or student a feeling of success and thereby promote self-esteem.

As parents and teachers, we know children have the amazing gift of curiosity. We can use that curiosity well by keeping reading time enjoyable. Therefore, when you work with your child or students on this book, captivate their interest by making the experience creative and positive. Read with them, listen to their comments and questions, and discuss the illustrations and examples provided. Especially do some experiments together. Have fun!

5

Stuff: A Good Place to Start

WOW! THE ANCIENT GREEKS THOUGHT A LOT ABOUT STUFF!

YEAH! AND THEY THOUGHT ABOUT A LOT OF STUFF, TOO!

It all started in Greece a very long time ago. People started wondering about the world around them. They asked, what kind of stuff makes up . . . well, stuff? What makes up clouds and rocks and woods and animals? How small can a piece of stuff be and *still be* . . . stuff?

The ancient Greeks asked many questions like these. They wanted to understand what **matter** was. Matter is the word **scientists** use for "stuff." Everything you can see—like the book you are reading, the table it is sitting on, and the chair *you* are sitting on—is matter. Many things you can't see are matter, too, like the air you're breathing right now.

What's Not Matter?

Do all of the pictures below show matter? Nope, one of them does not. Circle it.

Albert Einstein   idea   stuffed turkey    star

Well, the scientists from long ago came up with an **idea** about matter. That idea goes something like this:
If you cut something in half—say, a marble—then cut it in half again, then cut it in half again, and again, and again, sooner or later you'll cut it down to the smallest piece of marble possible. The Greeks called that smallest possible piece an **atom**. In Greek, *atom* means "can't be divided." And that was the whole idea. When you have a piece of matter that's so small you can't cut it into anything smaller, you have an atom.

> WHAT DO YOU THINK THIS MARBLE IS MADE OF, JUSTIN?

> ATOMS, ALEX. EVERYTHING IN THE WHOLE UNIVERSE IS MADE OF ATOMS.

> EXCEPT FOR YOUR BRAIN. THAT'S DEFINITELY MADE OF **MARBLES**!!

Try This!

How small can you cut the dotted rectangle of paper below. Carefully cut out the rectangle. Then try to cut as many pieces of paper from it as possible. When you can't cut any more pieces, check your skill by turning to the answers in the back of the book.

> CAN YOU CUT THE RECTANGLE INTO 50 PIECES? MORE? GIVE IT A TRY!

HOW MANY TIMES CAN YOU SAY, "HOW MANY PICKLED PARTICLES DID PETER PIPER PICK?"

If you guessed that atoms are so tiny your eyes can't see them, you are right. In fact, they're so tiny that *one million* hydrogen atoms connected together in a string would be only as thick as this page. That's amazing!

Now, there's no such thing as half an atom, but that doesn't mean there isn't stuff inside one. There is. The bits of matter inside atoms are called **particles**. We'll read more about them later. For now, let's stick with atoms. To understand what atoms *look like,* scientists draw pictures of them, like the ones on the top of page 9.

Searching for Matter

The words listed just below are all hidden in the puzzle. Find and circle them. The words can be up and down, across, or diagonal.

TABLE   PARTICLE
ROCK   WOOD
BOOK   ANIMAL
CLOUD   ATOM
PEOPLE FOOD

P	A	R	T	I	C	L	E
E	N	O	A	T	O	M	E
O	I	C	B	K	W	F	L
P	M	K	L	O	O	D	F
L	A	E	E	O	D	A	K
E	L	B	D	B	U	M	T
R	W	O	O	D	B	D	L

8

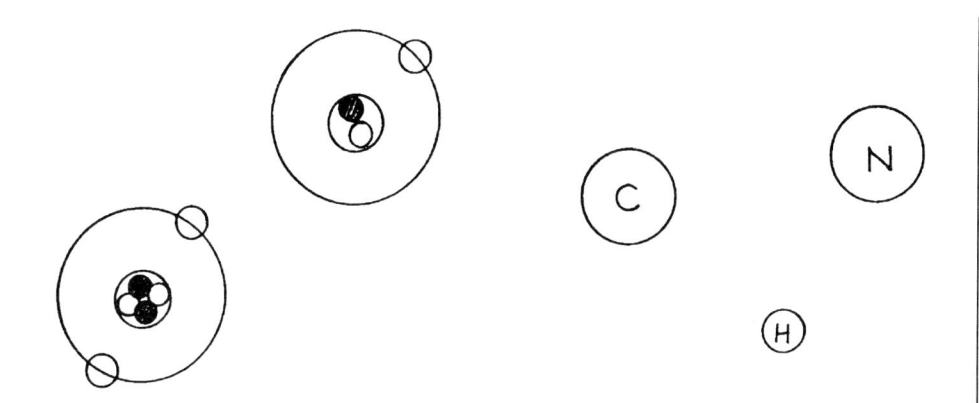

To understand atoms, they do **experiments**. An experiment is a kind of test to see how something works. The scientists build **models**, too. A model is made to show how something works.

Check Out the Science Words!

Do you remember reading about each of the words below? When you think you know the meaning of a word, put a ✓ in the box next to it.

- ❏ matter
- ❏ scientist
- ❏ idea
- ❏ atom
- ❏ particle
- ❏ experiment
- ❏ model

Secret Message, Part 1

Want to know a secret about particles? You'll have to circle every other letter in the puzzle below (and on the next page, too) to discover it. Begin circling with the second letter. Once you know Part 1 of the secret message, write it out on the blank lines provided.

MTPWXO SKTIYNPDNS NOMF IFMOLRPCFEHS
YPHLJANY BINMKPWOQRRTYAHNJT BRFOULRETS
UIBN GABTVOCMKSA.

_____

_____

_____

Now turn to Part 2 of the secret message!

Looking Deeper

WHAT'S THE MATTER, KARA?

MY BROTHER IS THE MATTER! WHEN HE SITS ON ME HE'S MORE MATTER!!

As mentioned before, the bits of matter inside an atom are called particles. These particles are called **protons**, **electrons**, and **neutrons**. Imagine how tiny they must be! After all, they're inside an atom, and an atom is *very* tiny.

Protons and electrons have something called **charge**. A charge is a quality that gives an atom electric and magnetic forces.

⇨ A proton has a **positive** charge. The sign we use for a positive charge is the plus (+) sign.

Secret Message, Part 2
Are you ready for the rest of the secret message? Circle every *third* letter in the puzzle, beginning with the *first* letter. Then write out the message below.

TECHXQERPY SOAKTRUVE
RZELULMSETVCONTIARPOIELC
ZSARTNEND OPNURUASCCOLMOETRABDR
CAFTUOCIRPACNIEPTS.

_____

_____

_____

⇨ An electron has a **negative** charge. The sign we use for a negative charge is the minus (-) sign.

⇨ A neutron has no charge. It's **neutral**. The sign we use for a neutral charge is zero.

Particle	Charge	How we draw it
proton	positive, +	⊕
electron	negative, –	⊖
neutron	neutral, o	Ⓞ

Protons and neutrons are packed tightly together, just like sardines in a can. The "can" they are in is in the exact center of the atom, at a place called the **nucleus**.

Pick Your Particle

In the atom shown below, you'll find the three different kinds of particles. Write the correct name on each blank, and answer the questions below.

How many electrons do you see? ____

How many neutrons? ____

What about protons? How many are there? ____

A lithium atom

Do you notice that the protons and neutrons are packed in the center of the atom? Where are the electrons? Describe where they are: _____

_____

11

Electrons are all by themselves, floating outside the nucleus. They revolve, or circle, around the nucleus, just the way our planets revolve around the sun.

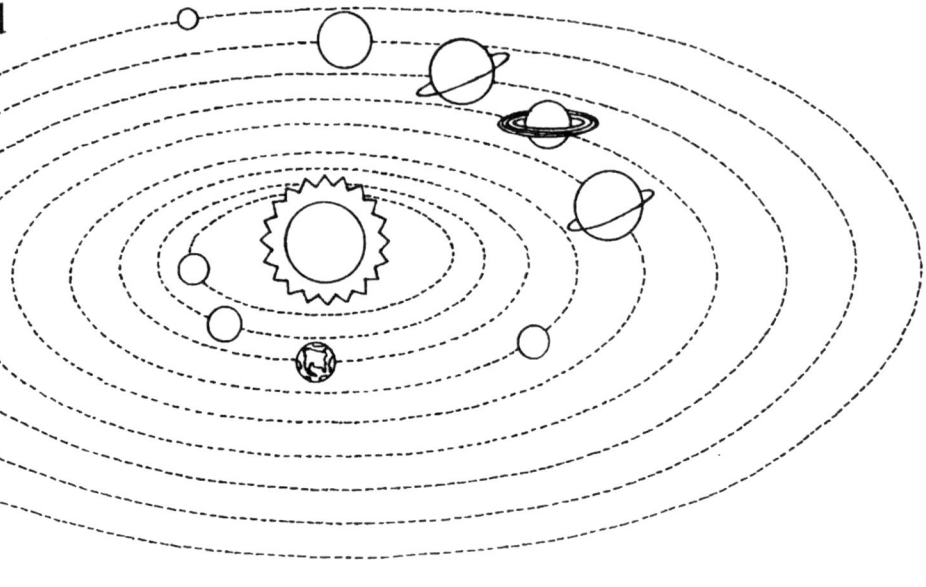

Now, anything that takes up space is matter. Anything that takes up space also weighs something. Different kinds of matter have different **weights**. That's something you

⇨ ⇨ ⇨ Go to page 15!

Hello, Helium

Below is another atom, and it's called helium. Helium is the gas used to blow up balloons. Each helium atom has two electrons, two protons, and two neutrons. Follow these directions:

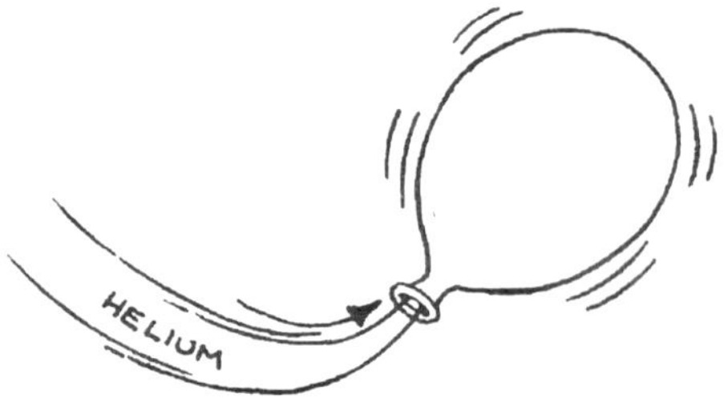

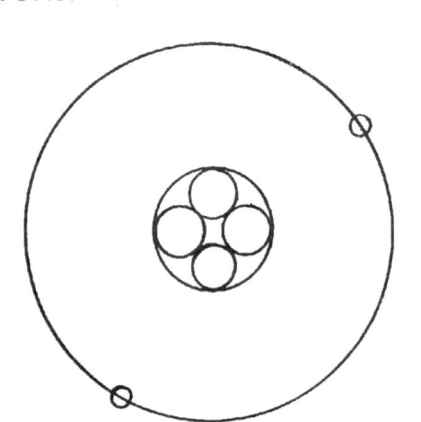

1. Color two protons red. Then, with a pen or pencil, draw a plus sign in each to stand for a positive charge.

2. Color two electrons green. Put a minus sign in each to stand for a negative charge.

3. Now fill in the neutrons. Draw them blue, and leave them empty to stand for a neutral charge.

EXPERIMENT: Charge It! C

Have you ever had static electricity in your hair? If you haven't, you're in for a treat. It looks really neat! Static electricity is a bunch of charges gathered together on an object. The charges are "static," which means they're not moving. (In electric current, charges move through a wire.) In static electricity, charges can switch objects. In the following experiment, you can make charges move from a balloon to your hair.

What you'll need:
- plastic of some kind (such as a plastic bag, a comb, or a balloon)
- wool clothing (such as a hat, mittens, or a sweater)
- mirror

What to do:
1. First, take whatever plastic item you choose and rub it on your hair. In this way, you "charge" the plastic.

2. Take the plastic away from your hair. What happens to your hair? Look in a mirror to see.

3. Now take a piece of wool clothing and rub it against your hair. What happens this time to your hair? Is it the same or different as when you rubbed the plastic against your hair?

What happened?
Normally, different objects have the same number of positive and negative charges on them. Sometimes, though, when you rub two objects together, some of the electrons from one object jump to the other object. For instance, if you rub your hair with a balloon, some of the electrons in your hair leak onto the balloon.

Turn the page for the rest of the experiment.

13

EXPERIMENT: Charge It! *(continued from page 13)*

That leaves your hair with more positive charges on it than negative charges, and it leaves the balloon with more negative charges than positive charges, as shown below.

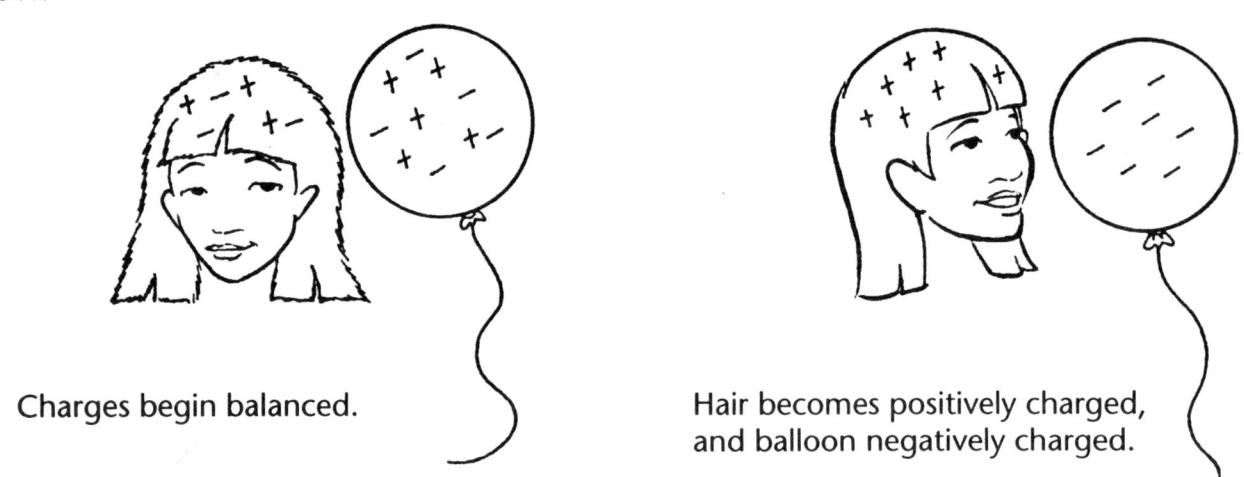

Charges begin balanced.

Hair becomes positively charged, and balloon negatively charged.

Positive and negative charges are opposite to each other. Being opposite, they move *toward* one another. Opposite charges *attract* each other. Same charges move *apart* or *repel* each other.

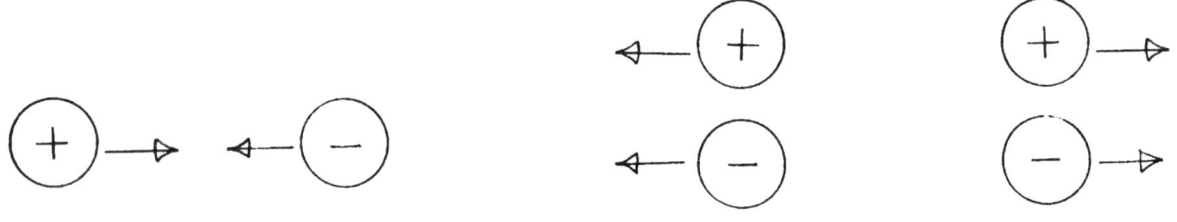

Opposite charges attract.

Same charges repel.

Since same charges repel, all the positive charges in your hair want to get away from each other. That causes your hairs to move as far apart as possible, and even stand straight up!

Extra! Extra!
If you want to prove that opposite charges attract each other, you can do the following: Charge some wool or plastic by rubbing it on your hair. (As you already know, your hair will start moving apart.) Now hold the wool or plastic over your hair and move it around above your head. Your hair will follow it! That's because the positive charges on your hair want to move closer to the negative charges on the wool or plastic.

What Do They Weigh?

electron 9×10^{-27} kilograms, or kg (20×10^{-27} lb)

proton 2×10^{-27} kg (4×10^{-27} lb)

ant 10^{-5} kg (2.2×10^{-5} lb)

dog (medium-sized) 10 kg (22 lb)

human (adult male) 100 kg (220 lb)

elephant 10,000 kg (22,046 lb)

blue whale 100,000 kg (220,462 lb)

Moon 7×10^{22} kg (15×10^{22} lb)

Earth 6×10^{24} kg (13×10^{24} lb)

Sun 2×10^{30} kg (4.4×10^{30} lb)

Milky Way Galaxy 2×10^{41} kg (4.4×10^{41} lb)

CHECK OUT THE SCIENCE WORDS!

Do you remember reading about each of the words below? When you think you know the meaning of a word, put a ✓ in the box next to it.

- ❑ proton
- ❑ electron
- ❑ neutron
- ❑ charge
- ❑ positive
- ❑ negative
- ❑ neutral
- ❑ nucleus
- ❑ weight

already know (who would you rather carry piggyback, your little sister or a 500-pound gorilla?!).

Compared to electrons, protons and neutrons are giant gorillas. As particles go, they're big and heavy. Electrons, on the other hand, are tiny and light. They add very little to an atom's weight. The weights of protons and neutrons add a lot to the atom's weight. In fact, they make up nearly all the weight of an atom.

THEY NEVER MET MY SISTER!

The two "gorillas" of an atom: the proton and the neutron

Here's an *Idea:* Do a Crossword!

So far in this book, you've come across a lot of words about science. These words appear in **bold**. Do you know what each one means?

Seven of those words appear in the crossword below. Read the clues, then fill in the puzzle. Good luck!

Across
3. Can't be divided

5. Test to see how something works

7. Matter inside atoms

Down
1. Gives electric and magnetic forces

2. Another word for stuff

4. Zero charge

6. Shows how something works

Here an Atom, There an Atom

Do you think you're ready to draw your own atoms? We'll start with something simple, then add a bunch of protons, neutrons, and electrons to really get you drawing!

A hydrogen atom

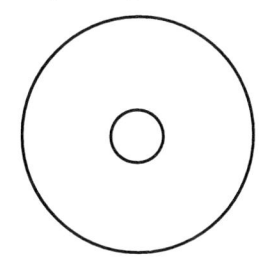

First, draw hydrogen. Hydrogen is the simplest atom. In its nucleus, it has only one proton and one neutron. Draw these. Outside the nucleus is one electron. Draw this.

A carbon atom

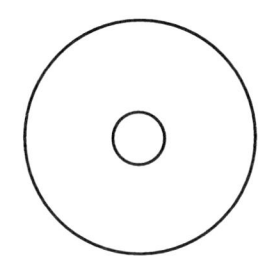

Next draw an atom with six protons and six neutrons in its nucleus. That's a carbon atom. Carbon also has six electrons. Draw these, too.

An oxygen atom

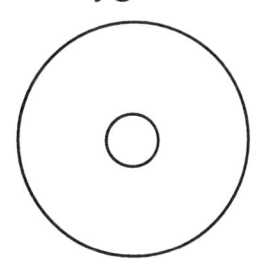

Here's a tough one! See if you can draw an oxygen atom. It has eight protons, eight neutrons, and eight electrons!

• • • cool facts • • •

⇨ **Hydrogen** is the most abundant substance in the universe. That means there is more hydrogen than any other kind of matter.

⇨ Plants and animals (including people) are sometimes called **carbon** life-forms. That's because we're all made of lots of carbon!

⇨ Did you know that nearly all life on Earth needs **oxygen** to survive?

Not All Atoms Are Alike!

IN FACT, WE KNOW OF MORE than a hundred different atoms. Each different kind of atom is called an **element**. Oxygen is an element. So are carbon, gold, silver, sodium, helium, krypton, chlorine, plutonium, and many, many others. What makes all the elements different from one another are the number of protons, neutrons, and electrons each has. Some elements, like hydrogen, are very light (it has only one proton in its nucleus). Others, like uranium, are very heavy (it has 92 protons in its nucleus!).

Do you remember that an atom's protons and neutrons make up nearly all of its weight? Sometimes, the same atom can have different weights. How is that possible?

Let's look at helium, the stuff used to fill balloons. Some helium atoms are normal, and some are, well, not so normal. While helium atoms *always* have two protons (that's why it *is* helium), they do *not* always have two neutrons. Some helium atoms have only one neutron; others have three or more neutrons. We call these not so "normal" helium atoms **isotopes**.

HERE'S A NORMAL HELIUM WITH 2 PROTONS AND 2 NEUTRONS IN ITS NUCLEUS.

HERE'S AN ISOTOPE HELIUM. IT HAS 2 PROTONS AND 4 NEUTRONS IN ITS NUCLEUS.

CHARGE!!!
Do you remember which charge belongs with which particle? The particles are shown below. Match particle with its correct charge. Then match each particle with its correct location.

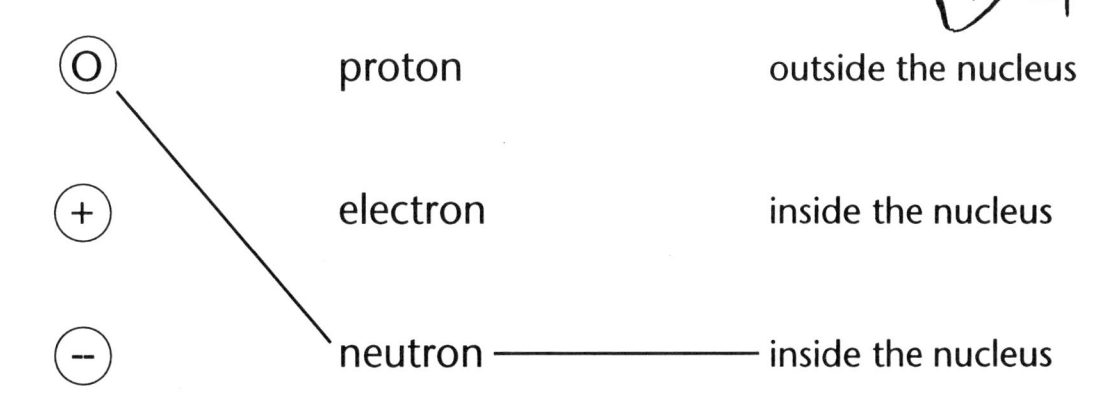

I COLORED AND DREW PARTICLES IN A PREVIOUS LESSON. THEN I FORGOT THE RULES.

(O)   proton   outside the nucleus

(+)   electron   inside the nucleus

(−)   neutron ———— inside the nucleus

19

"CALLING ALL HELIUM ISOTOPES! PLEASE STEP FORWARD!"

Here are three more isotopes of helium.

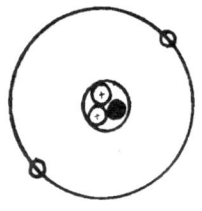

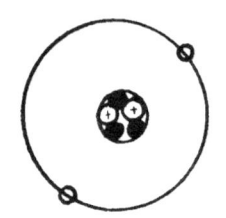

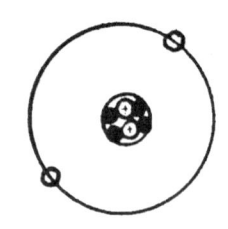

Did you notice how all the isotopes of helium have two protons? It's only the number of *neutrons* that changes to make different isotopes.

What does all this have to do with the weight of an atom? Neutrons and protons weigh about the same. So, when a helium

A Weighty Matter

The elements below all have different weights, some lighter than others, some heavier. Turn to the Periodic Table and find the weight of each element. Write it next to the element's symbol. When you have all the weights gathered, put the elements in order by weight, from lightest to heaviest.

element	symbol	weight	order by weight
oxygen	O	___	___
carbon	C	___	___
uranium	U	___	___
aluminum	Al	___	___
sulfur	S	___	___

isotope has one less neutron, it's lighter than normal helium. When a helium isotope has more neutrons, it's heavier than normal.

• • • don't forget the electrons! • • •
Normal helium atoms also have two electrons. When they do, the charge on the atom is neutral. Why? Because there are two *positive protons and* two *negative electrons. Two positives cancel out two negatives. The result? The helium atom is neutral.*

Speaking of electrons, what happens when the number of protons and electrons are *not* balanced? What happens when there are more electrons than protons? Or fewer electrons than protons? The answer is that the atoms get another name, **ions**.

Remember, an atom is usually neutral. That means it has the same number of electrons

---

Science Scramble
Learning all about science is easy. Unscrambling *words* about science is not! The scrambled words below can all be found in this book. If you need help, go back and re-read what you have learned. The first word is unscrambled for you.

mato	atom	ooptise	_____
cleeontr	_____	garceh	_____
oin	_____	norpto	_____
esstnciti	_____	trapelic	_____

Three of the words above have to do with charge. Put a star next to these.

21

and protons. But some atoms have only a weak hold on their electrons. They have very little electron-attracting power, so they easily lose one, two, or more of their electrons to other atoms nearby. With a loss of electrons, the atoms become positively charged ions. Ions with a positive charge are called **cations**.

Other atoms easily gain one or more electrons. They have lots of electron-attracting power. As a result, they steal electrons from nearby atoms and become negatively charged ions, or **anions**.

The charge on ions, such as the aluminum ion (Al^{3+}) or the sulfur ion (S^{2-}), is called the **oxidation number**. So, for Al^{3+}, the oxidation number is $^{3+}$. That number tells us how many electrons must be *added* to make the aluminum ion a neutral atom. Sulfur's oxidation number is $^{2-}$. That's how many electrons must be *removed* from the sulfur ion to make it a neutral atom.

If you want to pull electrons away from atoms in a science experiment someday, the process is called **oxidation**. Adding electrons to atoms is a process called **reduction**.

CHECK OUT THE SCIENCE WORDS!

Do you remember reading about each of the words below? When you think you know the meaning of a word, put a ✓ in the box next to it.

- ❏ element
- ❏ isotope
- ❏ ion
- ❏ cation
- ❏ anion
- ❏ oxidation number
- ❏ oxidation
- ❏ reduction

What Kind of Ion Is It?

By now you know that not all atoms are alike. Well, not all ions are alike either!

What If . . . ?

An atom has the *same number* of protons and electrons? ⇨ Then it's neutral.

An atom has *more* electrons than protons? ⇨ Then it's a negative ion (anion).

An atom has *fewer* electrons than protons? ⇨ Then it's a positive ion (cation).

So, how can you tell if an atom is neutral, negative, or positive? You compare the number of protons and electrons in it. Do that right now with the atoms below. Fill in the blank line under each with NEUTRAL, ANION, or CATION.

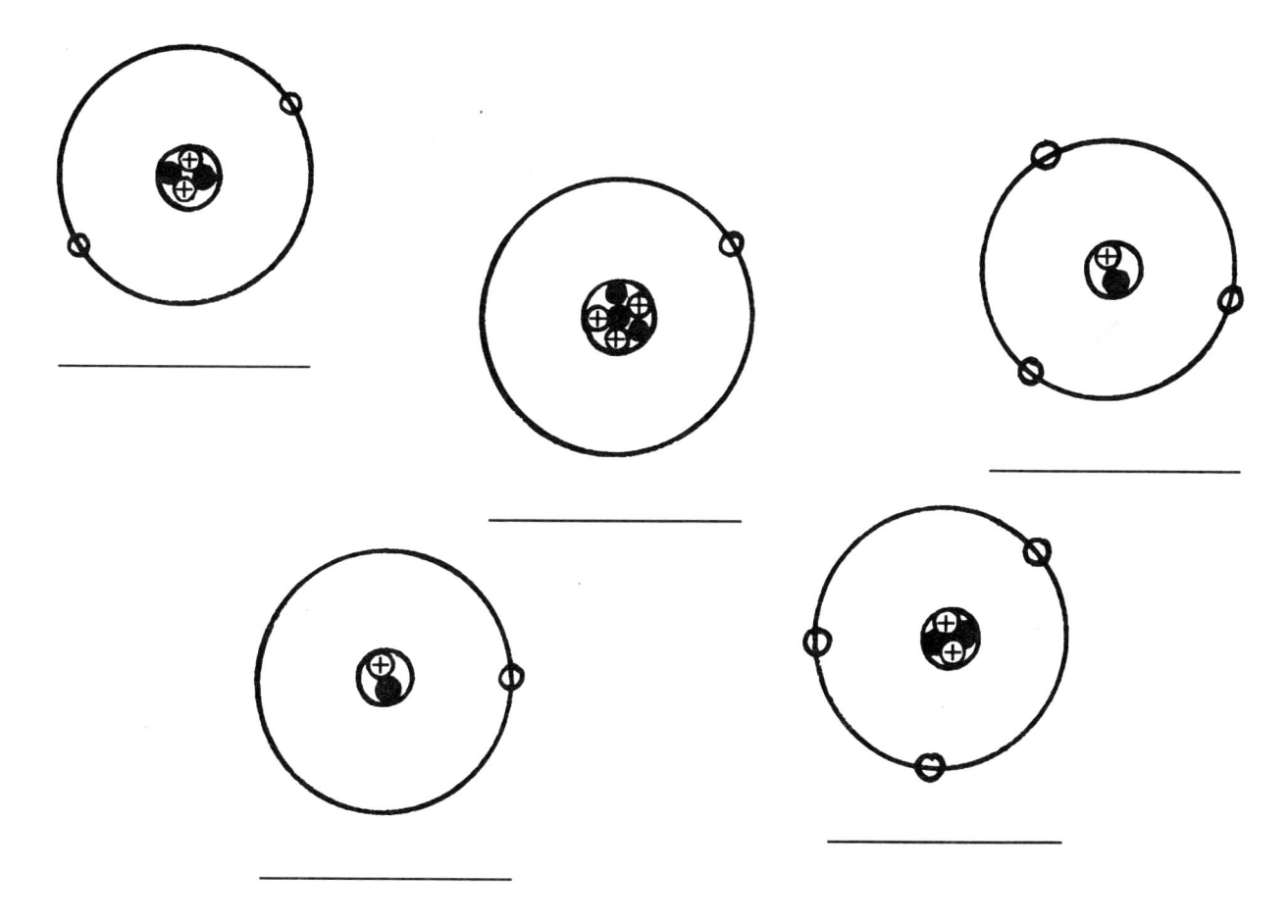

The Periodic Table

With more than a hundred different elements (109, to be exact), we could really use a way to look at them and compare them. Well, it turns out we do have a way! **The Periodic Table of the Elements** was created to organize all the elements in a way that made sense to people. It took many years to get the table just right. Different scientists from different countries worked on it. As new elements were discovered, the table was changed and improved. Today, the Periodic Table gives us a complete picture of all the elements.

	Group 1	Group 2	Group 3	Group 4	Group 5	Group 6	Group 7	Group 8
1	H=1							
2	Li=7	Be=9	B=11	C=12	N=14	O=16	F=19	
3	Na=23	Mg=24	Al=27	Si=28	P=31	S=32	Cl=35	
4	K=39	CA=40	— =44	Ti=48	V=51	CR=52	Mu=55	Fo=56, Co=59 Ni=59, Cu=63
5	(Cu=63)	Zn=65	— =68	— =72	As=75	Se=78	Br=80	
6	Rb=85	Sr=87	?Yt=88	Zr=90	Nb=94	Mo=96	— =100	Ru=104, Rb=104 Pd=106, Ag=108
7	(Ag=108)	Cd=112	In=113	Sn=118	Sb=122	Te=125	J=127	
8	Cs=133	Ba=137	?Di=138	?Ce=140	—	—	—	
9	(—)	—	—	—	—	—	—	
10	—	—	?Er=178	?La=180	Ta=182	W=184	—	Os=195, Ir=197 Pt=198, Au=199
11	(Au=199)	Hg=200	Ti=204	Pb=207	Bi=208	—	—	
12	—	—	—	Th=231	—	U=240	—	

Mandeleeve's Periodic Table of 1871

The Periodic Table of the Elements

1 H 1 Hydrogen																	2 He 4 Helium
3 Li 7 Lithium	4 Be 9 Beryllium											5 B 11 Boron	6 C 12 Carbon	7 N 14 Nitrogen	8 O 16 Oxygen	9 F 19 Fluorine	10 Ne 20 Neon
11 Na 23 Sodium	12 Mg 24 Magnesium											13 Al 27 Aluminum	14 Si 28 Silicon	15 P 31 Phosphorous	16 S 32 Sulfur	17 Cl 35 Chlorine	18 Ar 40 Argon
19 K 39 Potassium	20 Ca 40 Calcium	21 Sc 45 Scandium	22 Tl 48 Thallium	23 V 51 Vanadium	24 Cr 52 Chromium	25 Mn 55 Manganese	26 Fe 56 Iron	27 Co 59 Cobalt	28 Ni 59 Nickel	29 Cu 64 Copper	30 Zn 65 Zinc	31 Ga 70 Gallium	32 Ge 73 Germanium	33 As 75 Arsenic	34 Se 79 Selenium	35 Br 80 Bromine	36 Kr 84 Krypton
37 Rb 85 Rubidium	38 Sr 88 Strontium	39 Y 89 Yttrium	40 Zr 91 Zirconium	41 Nb 93 Niobium	42 Mo 96 *	43 Tc (97) Technetium	44 Ru 101 Ruthenium	45 Rh 103 Rhodium	46 Pd 106 Palladium	47 Ag 108 Silver	48 Cd 112 Cadmium	49 In 115 Indium	50 Sn 119 Tin	51 Sb 122 Antimony	52 Te 128 Tellurium	53 I 127 Iodine	54 Xe 131 Xenon
55 Cs 133 Cesium	56 Ba 137 Barium	57 La 139 Lanthanium	72 Hf 178 Hafnium	73 Ta 181 Tantalum	74 W 184 Tungsten	75 Re 186 Rhenium	76 Os 190 Osmium	77 Ir 192 Iridium	78 Pt 195 Platinum	79 Au 197 Gold	80 Hg 201 Mercury	81 Ti 204 Titanium	82 Pb 207 Lead	83 Bi 208 Bismuth	84 Po (209) Polonium	85 At (210) Astatine	86 Rn (-222) Radon
87 Fr (223) Francium	88 Ra 226 Radium	89 Ac 227 Actinium	104 Rf 261 *	105 Ha 262 Hahnium	106 Sg 263 *	107 Uns 262	108 Uno 265	109 Une 266	110 Uun 272 *								

58 Ce 140 Cerium	59 Pr 141 *	60 Nd 144 Neodymium	61 Pm (145) Promethium	62 Sm 150 Samarium	63 Eu 152 Europium	64 Gd 157 Gadolinium	65 Tb 159 Terbium	66 Dy 162 Dysprosium	67 Ho 165 Holmium	68 Er 167 Erbium	69 Tm 169 Thulium	70 Yb 173 Ytterbium	71 Lu 175 Lutetium
90 Th 232 Thorium	91 Pa 231 *	92 U 238 Uranium	93 Np 237 Neptunium	94 Pu (244) Plutonium	95 Am (243) Americium	96 Cm (247) Curium	97 Bk (247) Berkelium	98 Cf (251) Californium	99 Es (254) Einsteinium	100 Fm (257) Fermium	101 Md (258) *	102 No (259) Nobelium	103 Lr (260) *

25

Let's take a closer look at the Periodic Table . . .

Each element on the table has a name, a symbol, and a couple of different numbers. Look at hydrogen, in the upper left-hand corner of the table. The information inside a square tells you:

⇨ The element's name is hydrogen.

⇨ The large letter H is its **atomic symbol**. That's a short form of the name.

⇨ The number 1 is the **atomic number**. That number tells you how many protons are in hydrogen's nucleus.

⇨ The number 1 is the **atomic weight**. That's how much hydrogen weighs.

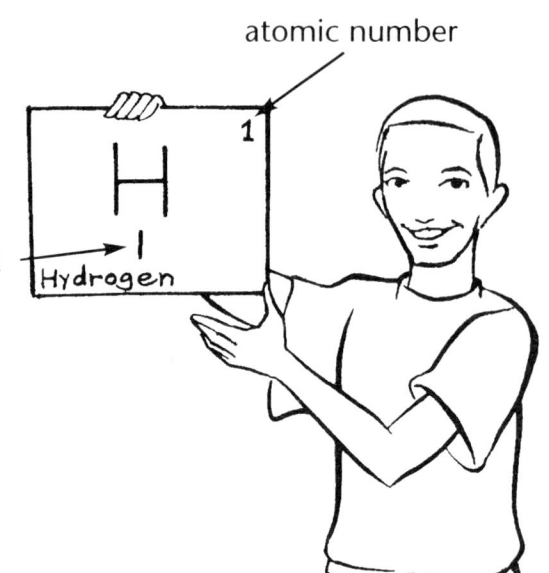

Read through all the element names on the Periodic Table. How many of them do you know already? On a piece of paper, write down all the elements whose names sound familiar to you.

• • • "without looking and trying" • • •

"Nothing, from mushroom to a scientific dependence, can be discovered without looking and trying."

Those words were spoken by a Russian chemist named Dmitry Mendeleev (1834–1907). In the 1860s, Mendeleev had a good idea—and then he looked and tried! He cut up a bunch of cards, and on each one he wrote the properties and atomic weight of an element. He did that for all the elements known at that time. Then Mendeleev arranged and rearranged the cards until he saw that there was a repeating (or periodic) pattern to the elements. That was very big news in the world of chemistry. Mendeleev's Periodic Table of the Chemical Elements, the very first one, was published in 1869.

Finish the Squares

Below are a bunch of element squares. But wait a minute—some information is missing! It's up to you to find the missing data on the Periodic Table and finish the squares. Here's how:

1. Each square contains at least one clue—a name, symbol, atomic number, or atomic weight. With the clue in hand, turn to the Periodic Table and find the correct square.

2. Copy the missing data onto the square below. Does that sound easy? Wait until you try it!

LOOK AT THE PERIODIC TABLE OF THE ELEMENTS TO HELP YOU.

• • • huh? • • •

It's easy to see how hydrogen or carbon or oxygen got their symbols. After all, H is short for hydrogen, C for carbon, and O for oxygen. But Na for sodium. What's that about? Each element has its own name, which is usually in English or Latin. Then, its one- or two-letter symbol is taken from its name . . . usually. *Sodium* is an English word, and its Latin name is *natrium*. Since the symbol S was already taken (by sulfur), chemists chose the symbol Na for sodium. Na is short for natrium.

How Did They Do That?

ARE YOU WONDERING HOW all the elements in the Periodic Table were put in the order they are? Why is the table set up the way it is? Just how *are* they arranged, and why aren't they in *alphabetical* order?! The activity on page 27 gave you some clues.

Have you figured it out yet?

As mentioned before, scientists worked for many years to create the Periodic Table we have today. At first, chemists arranged the elements by how they looked and acted. In other words, they focused on the elements' properties (you'll read more about properties in a few pages). In 1789, a chemist named Lavoisier tried to arrange the elements by how they combined with oxygen. It was a good start, because it got chemists thinking about how the elements acted.

Create-a-Table

Here's another fun way to get to know the Periodic Table of the Elements. Find each of the elements listed below, then fill in the blanks for atomic symbol, atomic number, and atomic weight. When you're through, answer the questions below the table.

Element Name	Atomic Symbol	Atomic Number	Atomic Weight
Fluorine	_____	_____	_____
Potassium	_____	_____	_____
Titanium	_____	_____	_____
Iron	_____	_____	_____
Nickel	_____	_____	_____
Krypton	_____	_____	_____
Lead	_____	_____	_____
Uranium	_____	_____	_____
Californium	_____	_____	_____
Einsteinium	_____	_____	_____
Mendelevium	_____	_____	_____

1. How many protons does fluorine have? ____
   How about krypton? ____

2. Which element is the heaviest? _____

3. When an atomic number goes up (as it does from fluorine to mendelevium), does the atomic weight also go up? ____

By the early 1860s, chemists began to look at atomic weight. Johann Wolfgang Dobereiner grouped elements that were chemically similar, then compared their weights. He and others began to see a pattern. Elements that had similar properties had weights that, roughly, were multiples of each other.

Then, in 1862, a major step was taken by a scientist named A. E. Beguyer de Chancourtois. The French chemist decided it made sense to look only at atomic weight, and he ordered the elements from lightest to heaviest. In doing that, it became clear to many chemists in different countries that there was a larger pattern to the elements' properties. As Mendeleev figured out, when the elements were arranged in a certain way, their properties repeated in an orderly pattern. He put the elements into seven rows (called **periods**). When he did that, the

---

Mystery Elements

Your mission, should you choose to accept it, is to discover the identities of the mystery elements on this page and the next. The only way to solve this mystery is by the elements' weights. Look at Mystery Element A. Mystery element A weighs exactly 1 atomic mass unit. That's your only clue. Search the Periodic Table to find out which element weighs exactly 1 atomic mass unit, then fill in the answer. Are you ready for your mission? Good luck!

Element A is

_____.

Element B is

_____.

See more mystery elements on the next page!

elements that were alike fell into up-and-down columns (called groups).

When Mendeleev published the Periodic Table in 1869, not all the elements were known. It had holes in it—places where elements that had yet to be discovered belonged. Mendeleev predicted that those mysterious elements would be found someday. When those elements finally were discovered, everyone could see how important and valuable the Periodic Table was.

CHECK OUT THE SCIENCE WORDS!

Do you remember reading about each of the words below? When you think you know the meaning of a word, put a ✓ in the box next to it.

❑ Periodic Table of the Elements
❑ chemistry
❑ atomic symbol
❑ atomic number
❑ atomic weight
❑ period

More Mystery Elements

Now you must conclude your mission by discovering the identities of the mystery elements below. Can you do it?

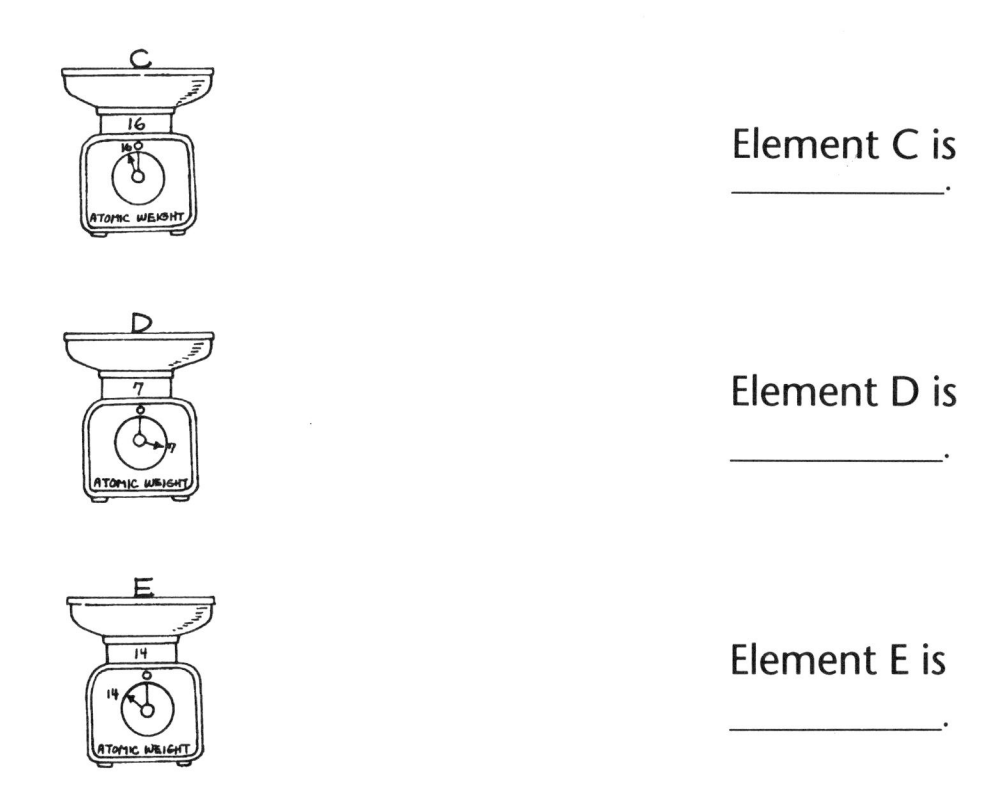

Element C is _____.

Element D is _____.

Element E is _____.

31

A Look at Properties

ONCE THE PERIODIC TABLE WAS ORGANIZED, it became clear to everyone: Elements in the same column, such as fluorine (F) and chlorine (Cl), were likely to look and behave the same way. They had similar **properties**. Elements that were beside each other in the same period, such as potassium (K) and calcium (Ca), also looked and behaved like each other. But elements far apart on the table, such as chlorine and potassium, were *nothing* like each other.

So, what are some of these properties? A few are listed below:

1. *Color:* Some of the elements can be identified by their color. For instance, bromine (Br) is brown, iodine (I) is violet, silicon (Si) is gray, and tin (Sn) is grayish-white.

2. *Reactivity to other chemicals:* Some elements react strongly to other chemicals, while others do not. Silicon isn't bothered by acids, but it is slowly attacked by bases. Tin is opposite to silicon; acids slowly attack it, but bases do not.

3. *Form (or state):* All matter comes in three different forms (gas, liquid or solid). Chlorine, for example, is a greenish-yellow gas. Mercury is a silvery liquid, and magnesium is a silvery solid at room temperature. (You'll learn more about solids, liquids, and gases later in this book.)

More About Silicon and Tin

Silicon, a nonmental, can be found in large supply in the Earth's crust. It's used together with other elements to make glass, computer chips, concrete, brick, and pottery.

Tin is a metal. It's soft and bendable, and it's used to coat other metals to prevent corrosion. (Corrosion is what happens when certain metals come in contact with the oxygen in air. Rust on a piece of iron is corrosion.)

GRID GAME: Can You Guess the Matter?

Each grid square below contains some properties that match one and only one of the substances at the bottom of the page. Which grid square goes with which substance? You decide! Then fill in the blank beside the substance. The first substance is done for you. When you're through with this guessing game, see what the real answers are at the back of the book.

	1	2	3	4
A	• colorless • odorless • gas at room temperatue • atomic weight 16	• lustrous white • metallic • soft, bendable • melts at 961°C • atomic weight 47	• crystallized carbon • hardest known substance • used as gemstone	• silvery-white • magnetic • extremely hard • melts at 1535°C • atomic weight 56
B	• colorless • lightest of all gases • melts at -259°C • atomic weight 1	• reddish-brown • metallic • excellent heat conductor • atomic weight 29	• silvery-white • metallic, liquid at room temperature • melts at -39°C • atomic weight 200	• grayish-black solid • corrosive and poisonuos • melts at 113.5°C • atomic weight 127

iodine   __B4__

silver   _____

copper   _____

iron   _____

hydrogen   _____

oxygen   _____

diamond   _____

mercury   _____

CHECK OUT THE SCIENCE WORDS!

Do you remember reading about each of the words below? When you think you know the meaning of a word, put a ✓ in the box next to it.

❑ properties

4. *Melting point:* Each element has its own temperature at which it melts from a solid to a liquid. For silicon, that temperature is 1410°C. For tin, the melting temperature is 232°C.

5. *Hardness:* Pure gold is a beautiful, shiny-yellow metal, but it's fairly soft, easily scratched, and bendable. To make it hard enough for rings and bracelets, people have to add other, harder metals to it. Iron, another metal, is naturally very hard. It won't bend or scratch easily, so it's useful for building things.

What Am I?

Can you solve the riddles? Give it a try! (If you need help, go back and review the science words on pages 6, 7, 18, and 21.)

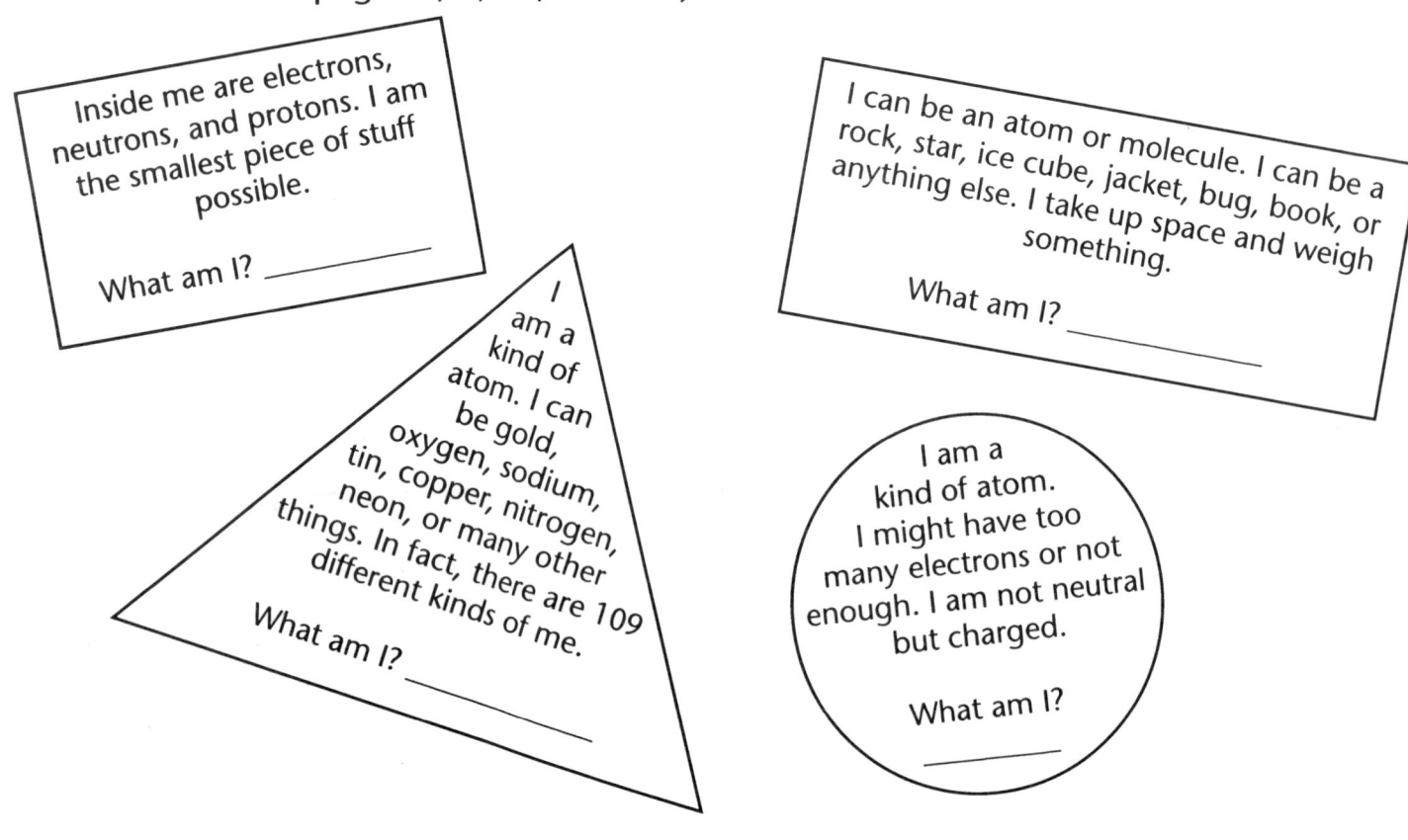

Inside me are electrons, neutrons, and protons. I am the smallest piece of stuff possible.

What am I? _____

I can be an atom or molecule. I can be a rock, star, ice cube, jacket, bug, book, or anything else. I take up space and weigh something.

What am I? _____

I am a kind of atom. I can be gold, oxygen, sodium, tin, copper, nitrogen, neon, or many other things. In fact, there are 109 different kinds of me.

What am I? _____

I am a kind of atom. I might have too many electrons or not enough. I am not neutral but charged.

What am I? _____

The Atomic Shell Model

SO FAR IN THIS BOOK, we've talked a bit about neutrons, and we've talked a lot about protons and atomic numbers. But we keep forgetting the electrons! Before we go any further in our study of atoms, let's turn to some really important ideas about electrons.

Have you wondered *why* the elements look different from each other? Or why some boil at a low temperature and others at a high temperature? A lot of the properties of the elements can be explained by the **Atomic Shell Model**.

> A MODEL, AS YOU KNOW, IS A WAY OF LOOKING AT AN IDEA.

> SCIENTISTS BUILD MODELS TO HELP THEM UNDERSTAND THEIR IDEAS.

••• what's in a name? •••

Why is the Atomic Shell Model called that? First of all, it's a set of ideas involving a **model**. *(A* **model***, as you know, is a tool scientists use to help them understand their ideas.) This particular model is of an atom and its electrons shells—or,* **atomic shells***. That's why it's called the Atomic Shell Model.*

Understanding the Atomic Shell Model is really all about looking at where electrons are as they float around the nucleus. By "shell," think of a closed ball, sort of like an eggshell. Now imagine that instead of just one shell, you have layers of them, one inside the other. Each layer of shell is like a ball inside another ball, which is inside still another ball.

On each shell, there are grooves that can hold electrons. One electron can fit into each groove. When all the grooves in a shell are filled up, that shell is said to be closed.

Electrons can move from one groove to another groove. They can move within the same shell, or they can jump from one shell to another.

Memory Game

Below are the atomic shell models of several elements. Their names are printed for you. When you think you can remember all the elements below, turn the page.

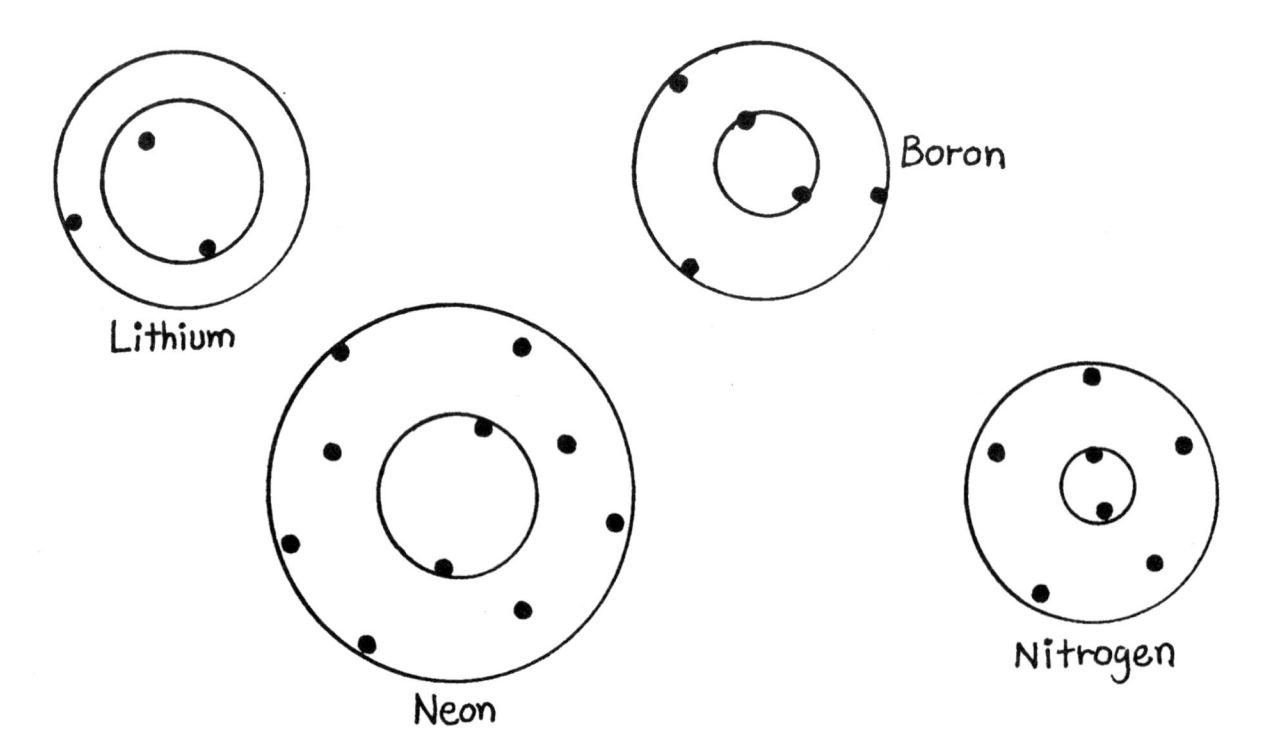

Lithium

Boron

Neon

Nitrogen

36

A little earlier, we said that a lot of the elements' properties can be explained by the Atomic Shell Model. When two elements are alike in the way their shells *are filled,* the elements *act* alike. Take a look at sodium and potassium.

The two elements are very similar. Why? Do you see how both sodium and potassium have closed *inner* shells? More important, can you see how their outermost shell has only one electron in it? Now, sodium has just one filled inner shell and potassium has *two,* but that doesn't matter. What makes sodium

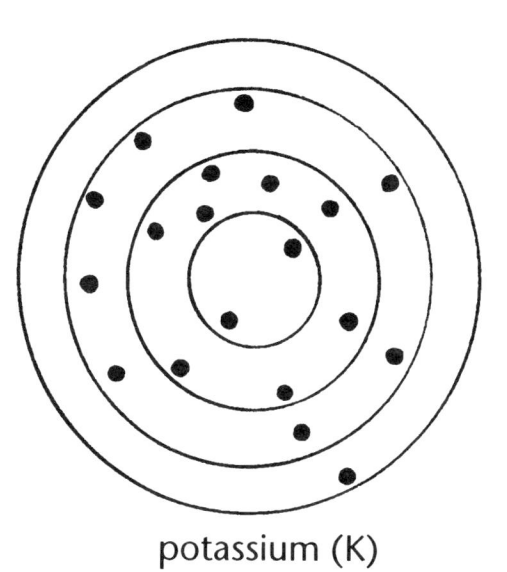

sodium (Na)

potassium (K)

Memory Game   *(continued from page 36)*
Now fill in the blanks with the correct names of the elements. If you need help, go back to page 36 and study some more!

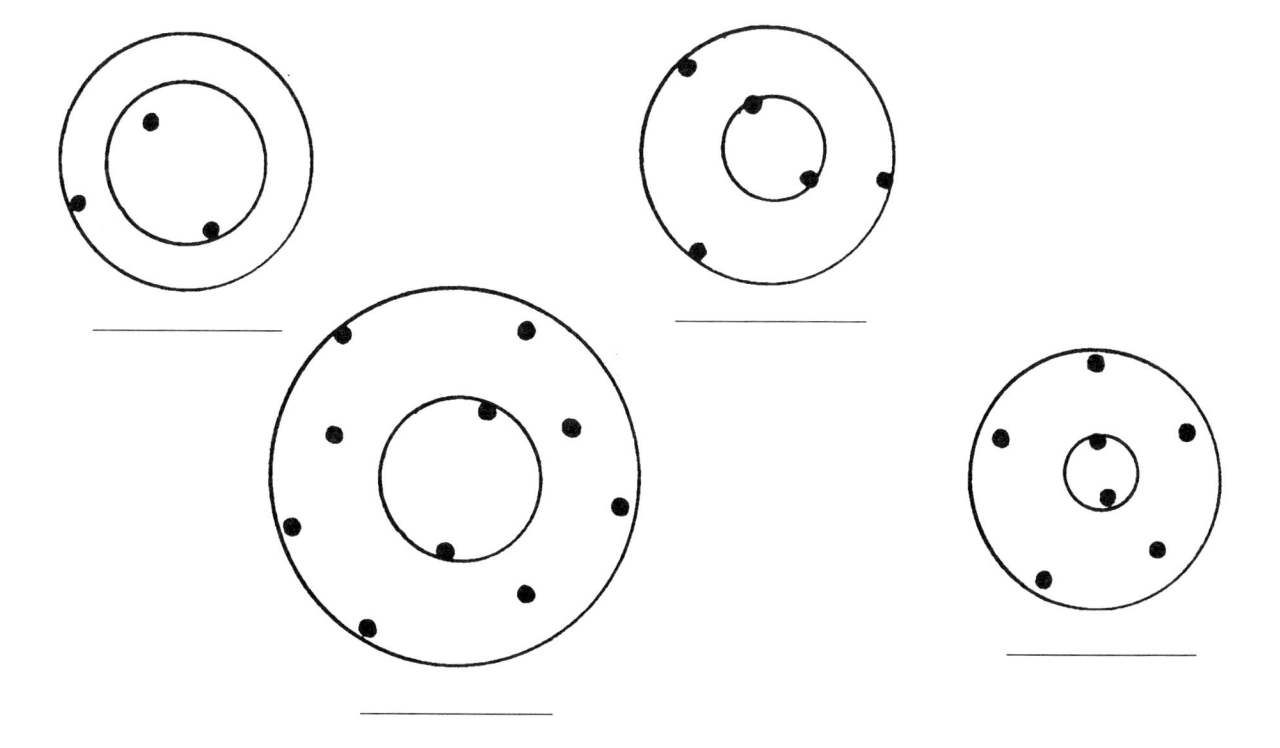

37

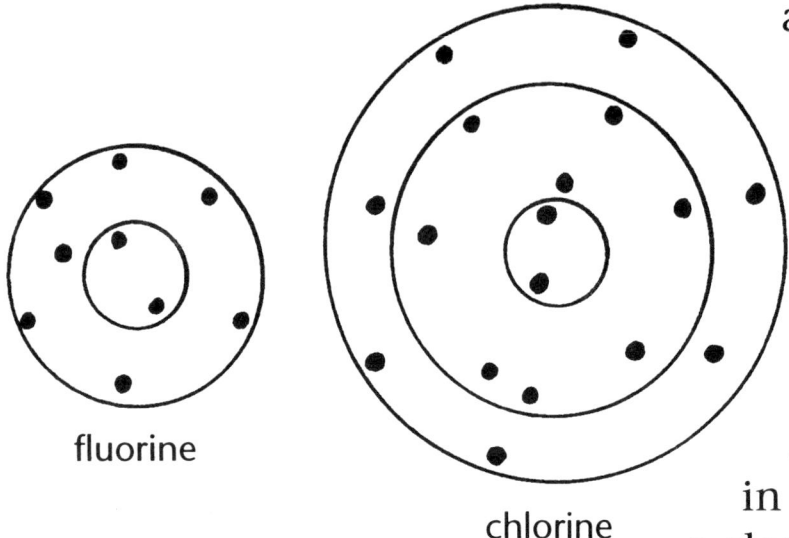

and potassium so much alike is the one electron in their outside shells. Pretty cool! Let's now examine two elements from all the way on other side of the Periodic Table: fluorine and chlorine. Both fluorine and chlorine have seven electrons in their outermost shell. To have a closed shell, each atom needs one more electron.

fluorine

chlorine

Shape Code
Use the shape code below to help you discover something about electrons.

A	B	C	D	E	F	G	H	I	J	K	L	M
◗	★	©	✈	❀	✕	☞	♥	✎	▼	✉	☆	✳

N	O	P	Q	R	S	T	U	V	W	X	Y	Z
☞	▲	◆	❖	✧	✪	☀	✿					

E L E C T R O N S   M A K E   E A C H

E L E M E N T   U N I Q U E.★

E L E C T R O N S   R U L E!

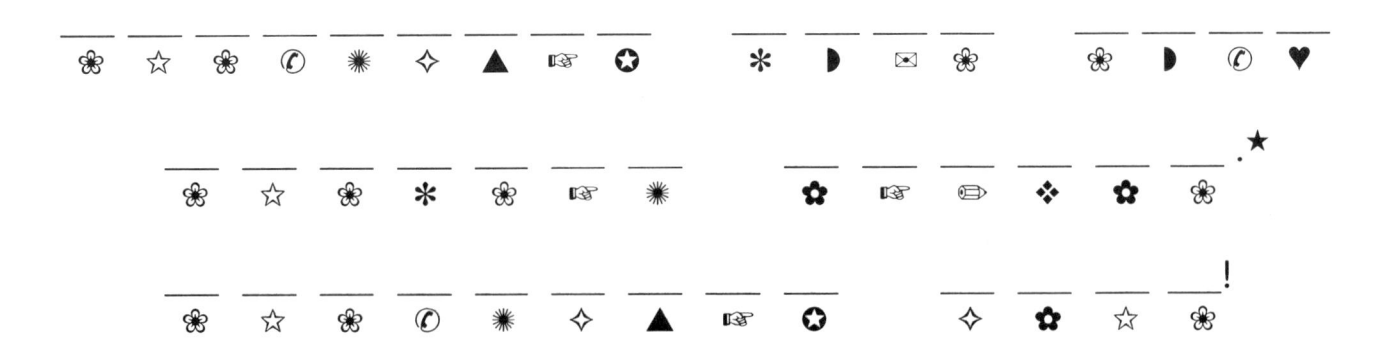

★This word means "one of a kind."

Which Is Like What?

From the way their shells are filled, sodium (Na) and potassium (K) are alike (remember the pictures on page 37?). Chlorine (Cl) and fluorine (F) are similar, too. Below are a couple more pairs of elements that are like each other. Match them up, then fill in the blank lines.

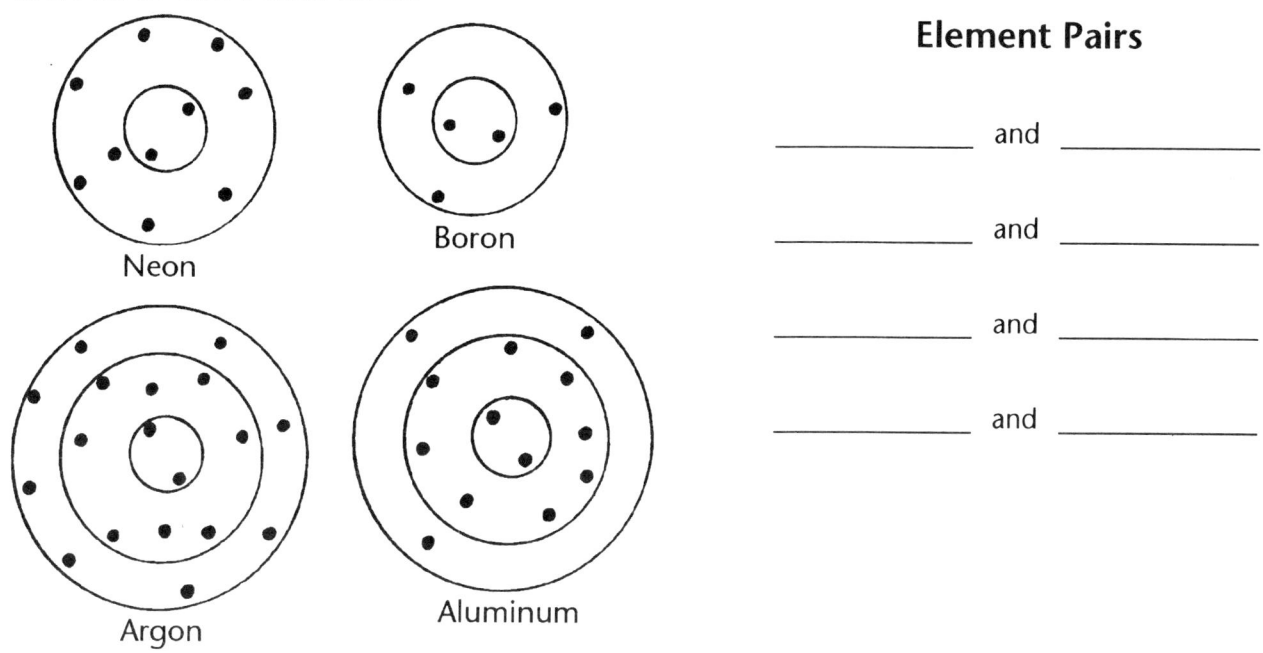

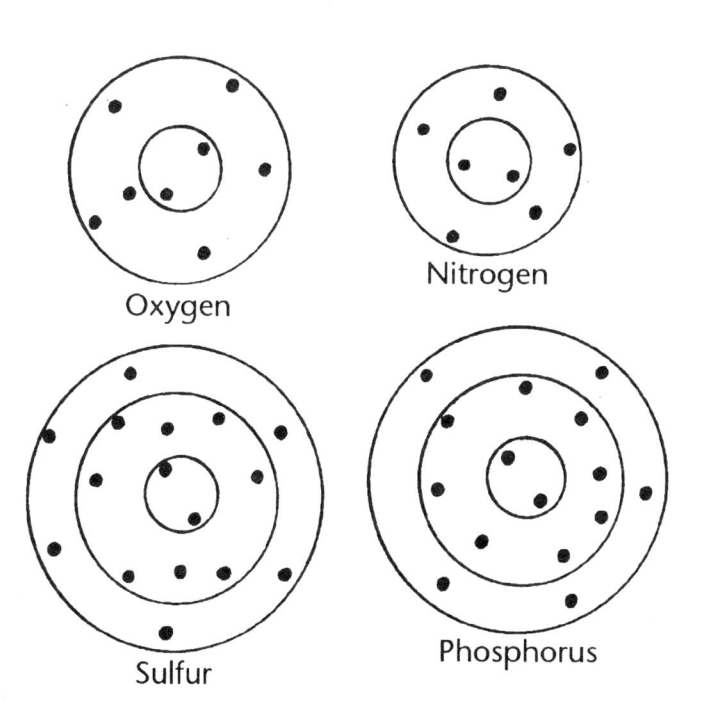

Neon

Boron

Argon

Aluminum

Oxygen

Nitrogen

Sulfur

Phosphorus

Element Pairs

_____ and _____

_____ and _____

_____ and _____

_____ and _____

CHECK OUT THE SCIENCE WORDS!

Do you remember reading about each of the words below? When you think you know the meaning of a word, put a ✓ in the box next to it.

❑ **Atomic Shell Model**

39

They'd Rather Be Charged

Some elements are not very happy when they're neutral. They gain or lose electrons instead. Let's follow the process with two different elements, flourine and lithium.

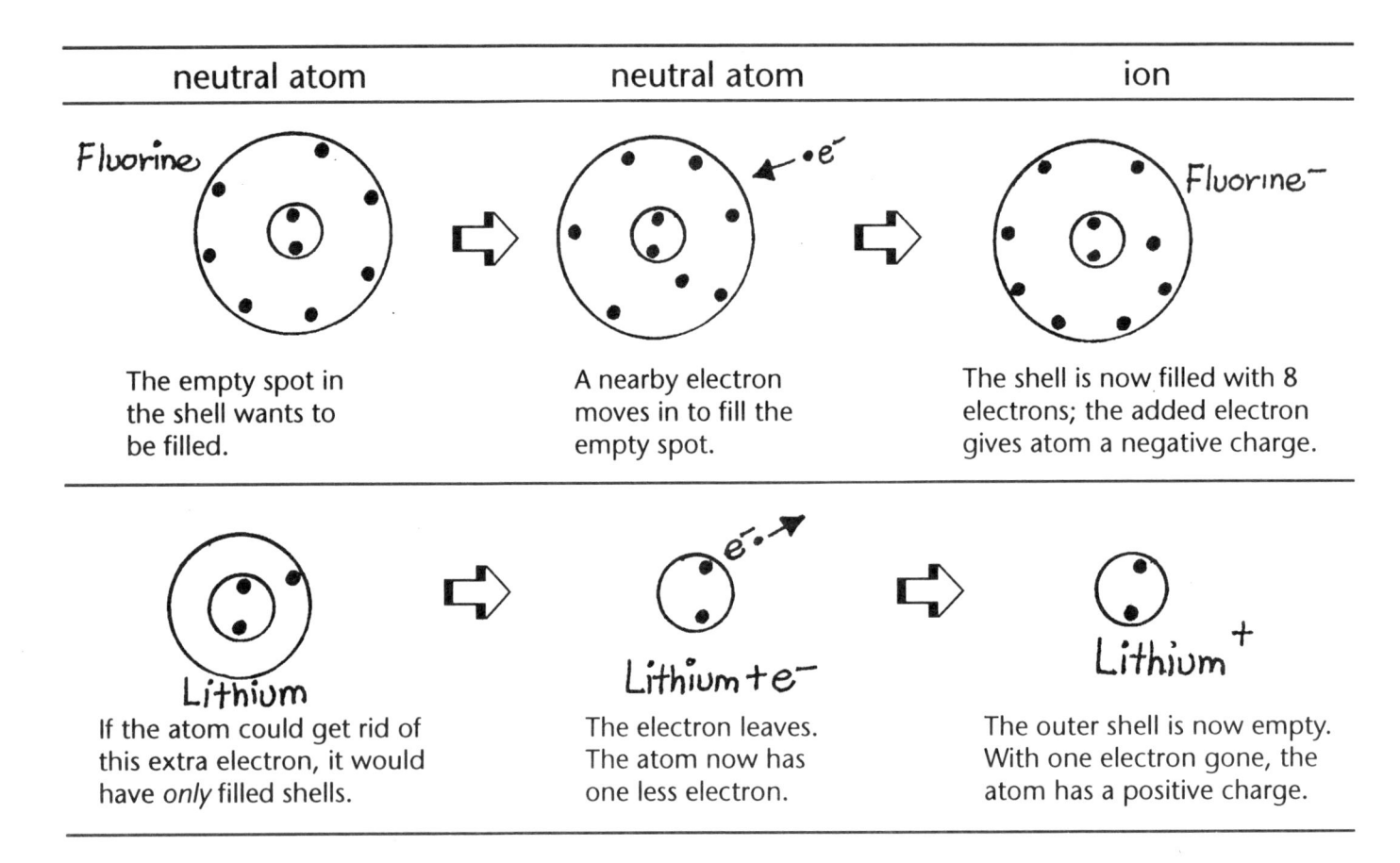

neutral atom	neutral atom	ion

Fluorine (first diagram): The empty spot in the shell wants to be filled.

A nearby electron moves in to fill the empty spot.

The shell is now filled with 8 electrons; the added electron gives atom a negative charge. (Fluorine⁻)

Lithium: If the atom could get rid of this extra electron, it would have *only* filled shells.

Lithium + e⁻: The electron leaves. The atom now has one less electron.

Lithium⁺: The outer shell is now empty. With one electron gone, the atom has a positive charge.

Now it's your turn. Look carefully at each element below and decide if it would be happier to ① stay as it is; ② gain electron(s) and become negative; or ③ lose electron(s) and become positive. Put a ①, ②, or ③ beside each atom.

Oxygen ○   Lithium ○   Beryllium ○

40

Connecting Atoms

WHEN TWO OR MORE ATOMS connect together, what do you think you get? You get a **molecule**! A great example of a molecule is something you drink everyday, and bathe with, too: water.

In a molecule of water, a hydrogen atom is connected to an oxygen atom, which is connected to a second hydrogen atom. Another way of looking at it is that an oxygen atom is connected to two hydrogen atoms. The connections are called **bonds**.

Because water is made of *two* atoms of hydrogen and *one* atom of oxygen, we shorten it and say H_2O. (We don't have to say H_2O_1, because it's understood there's just one atom of oxygen.) H_2O is the **molecular formula** for water. A molecular formula is really just a recipe. How do you make one molecule of water? Take two atoms of hydrogen and mix them with one atom of oxygen. Presto—water!

Here's a more complicated molecule, called octane. Its formula is C_8H_{18}.

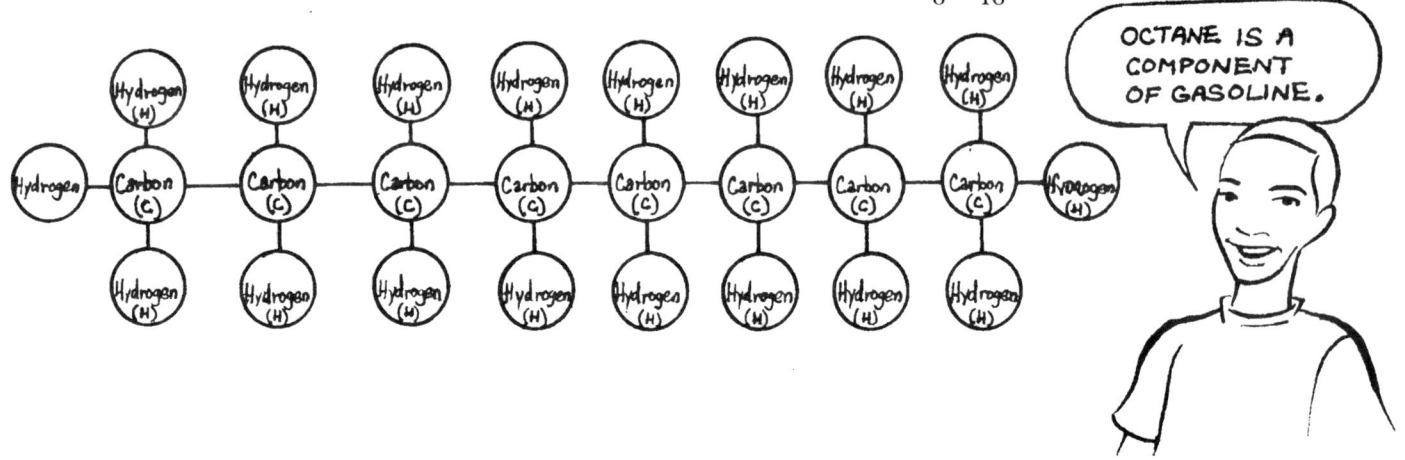

OCTANE IS A COMPONENT OF GASOLINE.

⇨ How many carbon atoms are there? ____

⇨ How many hydrogen atoms? ____

⇨ How many bonds? ____

Color the Compound: Part 1

Ammonia is another molecule. We use ammonia to clean stuff with. It's also used as a plant fertilizer, because plants need nitrogen to be healthy. The molecular formula for ammonia is NH_3. The nitrogen (N) atom is at the center of the molecule, and the three hydrogen (H) atoms are connected to it. The H atoms are not connected to each other, only to the N atom.

BE A GOOD PLANT AND TAKE ALL YOUR NITROGEN.

The ammonia molecule shown here needs to be finished.

⇨ Color the H atoms blue.

⇨ Color the N atom green.

⇨ Draw three black bonds connecting the N atom to the H atoms.

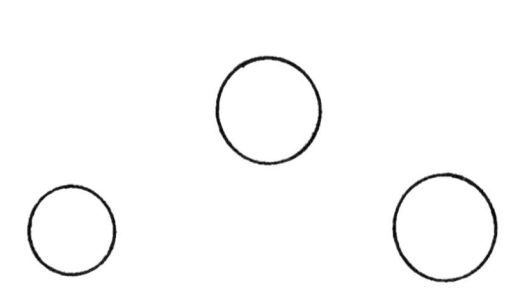

You can color another compound on the next page!

Just as elements can look different from each other, so can molecules.

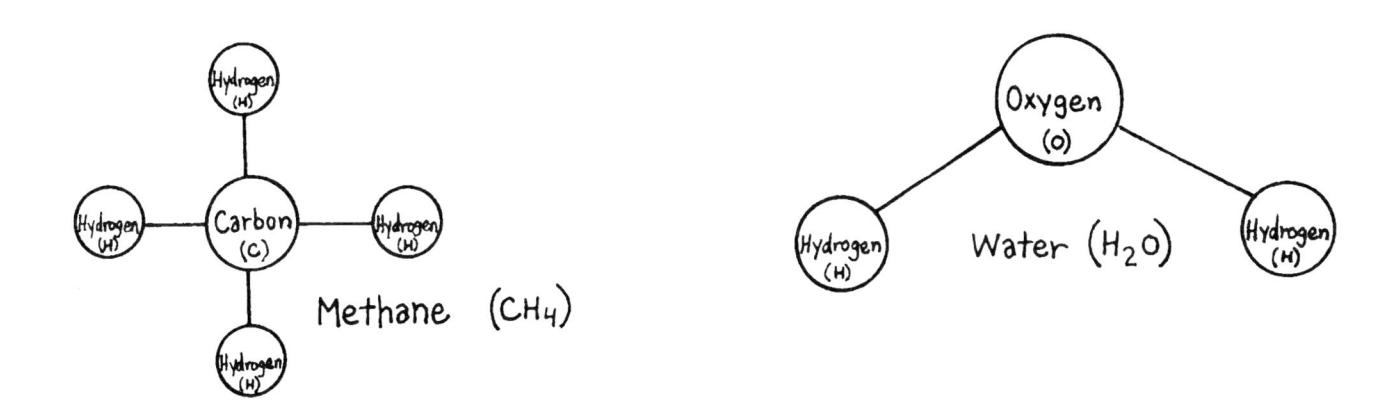

Methane (CH₄)

Water (H₂O)

Every molecule has a different weight, too. Some are simple and light, such as water (H₂O). Others, like octane (C₈H₁₈) are larger and heavier. The weight of a molecule is ⇨ ⇨ ⇨ *Go to page 45!*

Color the Compound: Part 2

Calcium carbonate is found as chalk, limestone, and marble. Long ago, the calcium made up the shells and skeletons of marine organisms. Then, over time, it became calcium carbonate. Today it's used to make ordinary chalk, medicines, and paste for cleaning teeth! The molecular formula for calcium carbonate is CaCO₃. The carbon (C) atom is at the center of the molecule, and the calcium (Ca) and three oxygen (O) atoms are connected to it.

The calcium carbonate molecule below needs to be finished.

⇨   Color the Ca atom red.

⇨   Color the C atom yellow.

⇨   Color the O atoms brown.

⇨   Draw three black bonds connecting the C atom to the Ca and O atoms.

Count 'Em Up!

Count up each kind of atom in the molecules below and on the next page. Then fill in the blanks to see what the molecules' formulas are. The first one is done for you.

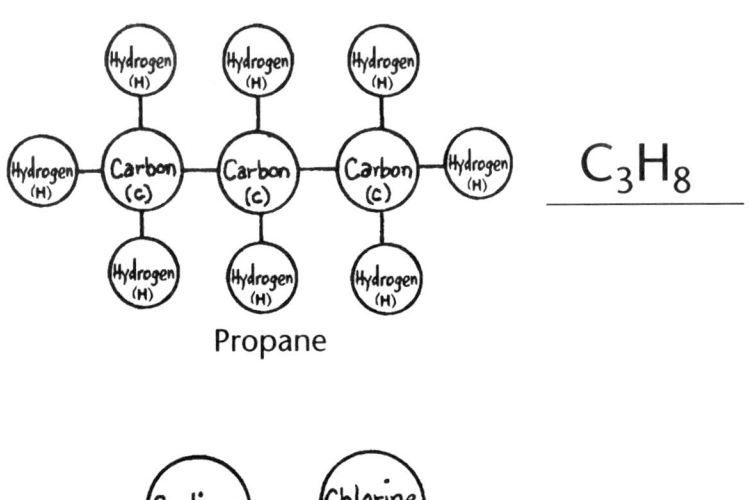

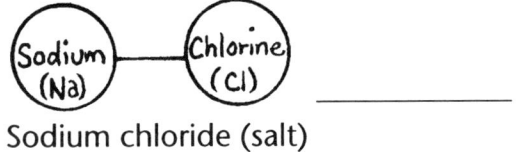

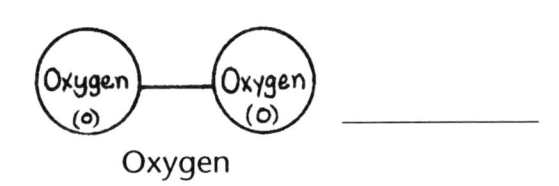

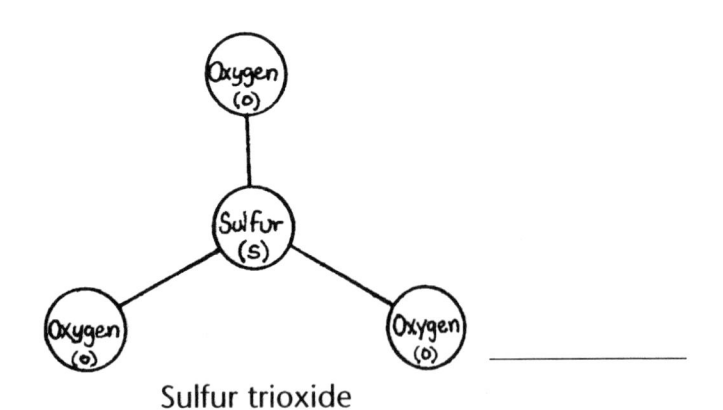

C_3H_8

Propane

ALL THE REST ARE DONE FOR YOU TOO... IN INVISIBLE INK.

Sodium chloride (salt)

Oxygen

Sulfur trioxide

44

called, simply enough, **molecular weight**. If you add up the weight of all the atoms in a molecule, you get the molecular weight.

Let's figure out the weight of something simple. The salt you sprinkle on your French fries is a molecule called sodium chloride, and its molecular formula is NaCl. Its recipe is one atom of sodium (Na) plus one atom of chlorine (Cl).

	weight
one atom of Cl:	35
one atom of Na:	+ 23
total:	58

So, the molecular weight of NaCl is 58.

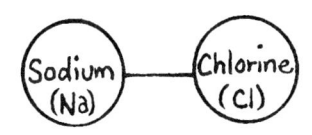

Double the Words

Do you see the seven science words in the box on the bottom of the next page? You can mix and match them with different word endings to create all new words (in fact, you can *double* the number of words, from seven to fourteen). You'll find word endings in the other box on the next page. To create a word, solve each of the "math" problems below. Here's an exampe of a harder one:

$$4 - e + A = \underline{}$$

Science Word 4 is "isotope."   Take away the e from "isotope."   Add Word Ending A, "ic."   =   isotopic

"Math" Problems

Once you make a new word, write it in a blank box on the next page.

1. 1 + B
2. 7 + B
3. 4 + B
4. 2 + F
5. 3 + A
6. 5 + B
7. 2 + B
8. 1 + A
9. 3 + B
10. 7 − ce + E
11. 6 − us + C
12. 7 − ce + D
13. 5 − e + C

45

CHECK OUT THE SCIENCE WORDS!

Do you remember reading about each of the words below? When you think you know the meaning of a word, put a ✓ in the box next to it.

- ❑ **molecule**
- ❑ **bond**
- ❑ **molecular formula**
- ❑ **molecular weight**

Another simple (and much lighter) molecule is water, H_2O.

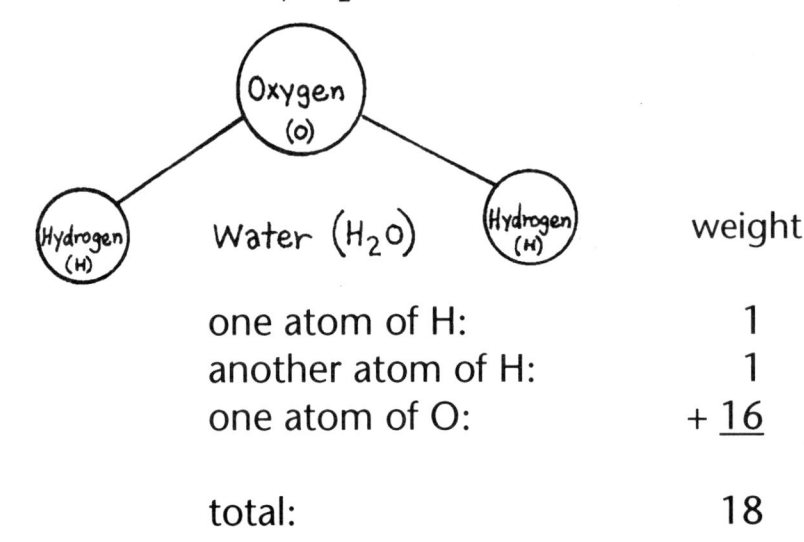

Water (H_2O)

	weight
one atom of H:	1
another atom of H:	1
one atom of O:	+ 16
total:	18

You can figure out the molecular weights of a few other molecules (more complicated ones!) in the activity on the next page.

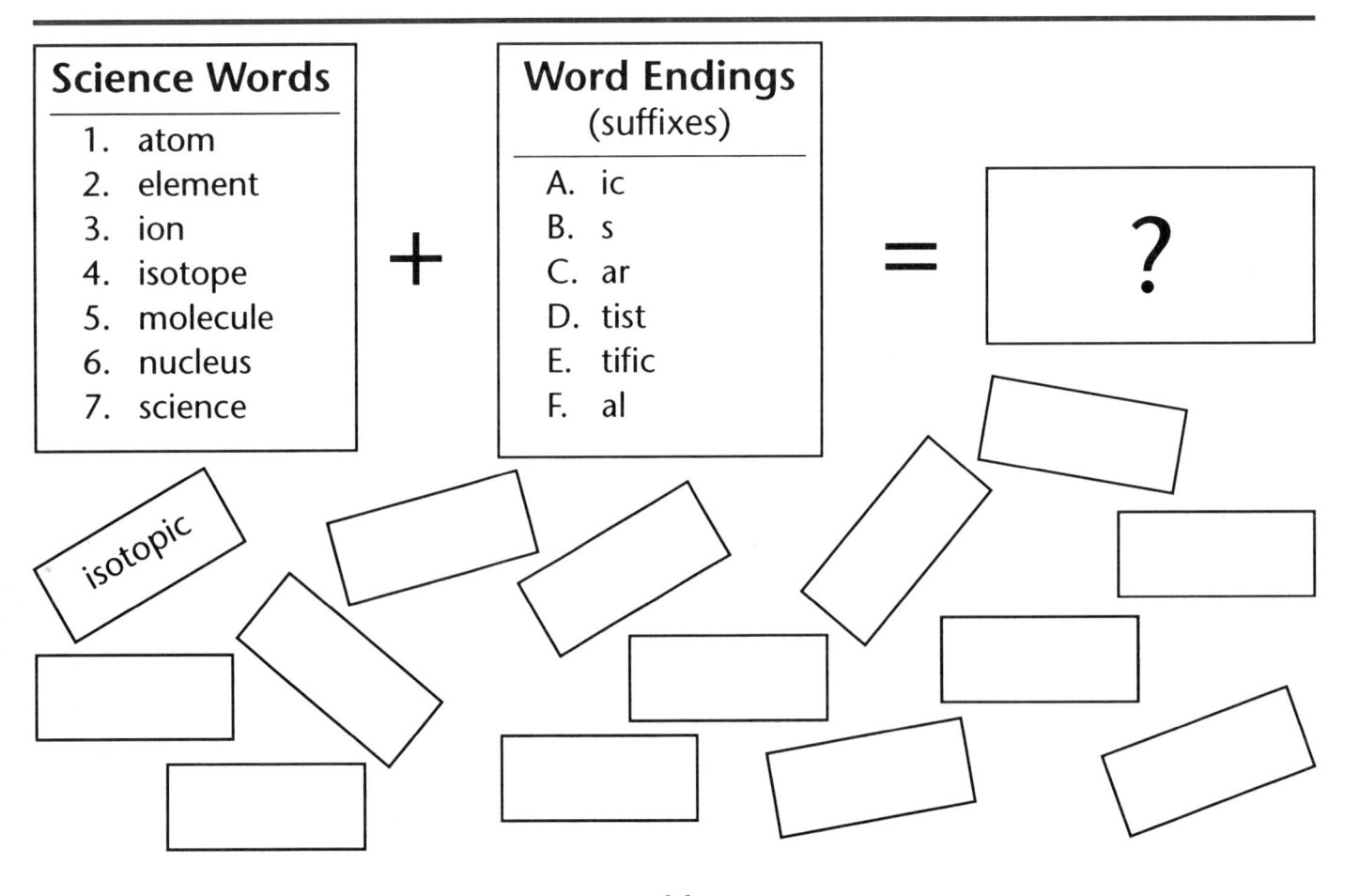

Science Words
1. atom
2. element
3. ion
4. isotope
5. molecule
6. nucleus
7. science

+

Word Endings
(suffixes)

A. ic
B. s
C. ar
D. tist
E. tific
F. al

= ?

isotopic

46

How Much Do They Weigh?

Below are a bunch of different molecules, some simple, some more complex. Find out how much each one weighs by adding up their atomic weights. You can find these weights in the Periodic Table on page 25. The first one is done for you.

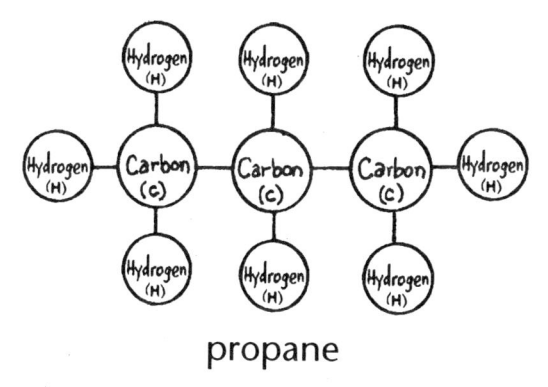

propane

Step 1: Propane has __3__ atoms of carbon.
Each carbon weighs __12__.
3 x 12 = 36   __36__

Step 2: It also has __8__ atoms of hydrogen.
Each hydrogen weighs __1__.
8 x 1 = 8   __8__

Total: __44__

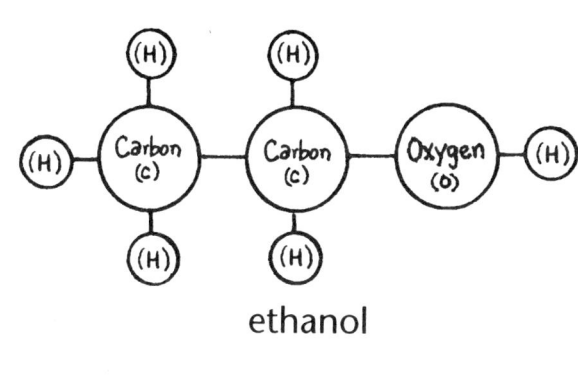

ethanol

Step 1: Ethanol has ___ atoms of carbon.
Each carbon weighs ___.
___ x ___ = ___   _____

Step 2: It also has ___ atoms of hydrogen.
Each hydrogen weighs ___.
___ x ___ = ___   _____

Step 3: Finally, it has ___ atom of oxygen.
Each oxygen weighs ___.

___ x ___ = ___   _____

Total: _____

PROPANE IS ALSO CALLED NATURAL GAS. WE USE IT AS FUEL.

AND, OF COURSE, THE COMMON NAME FOR ETHANOL IS "DRINKING ALCOHOL."

You'll find more molecular weights to add up on the next page!

How Much Do They Weigh?

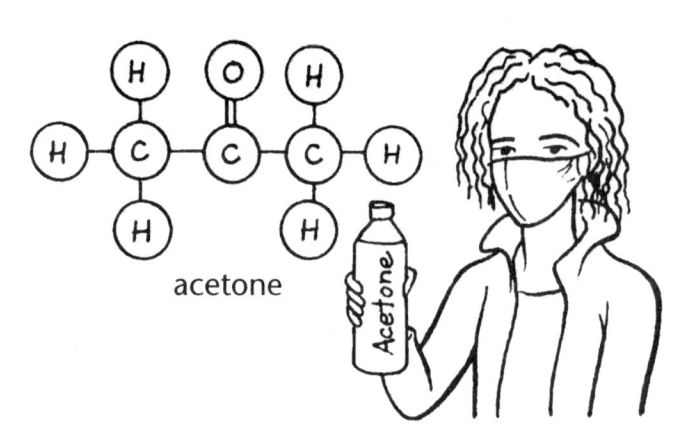

Step 1: Acetone has ___ atoms of carbon.
Each carbon weighs ____.
___ x ___ = ___   _____

Step 2: It also has ___ atoms of hydrogen.
Each hydrogen weighs ____.
___ x ___ = ___   _____

Step 3: Last, acetone has ___ atom of oxygen. Each oxygen weighs ____.
___ x ___ = ___   _____

Total: _____

acetone

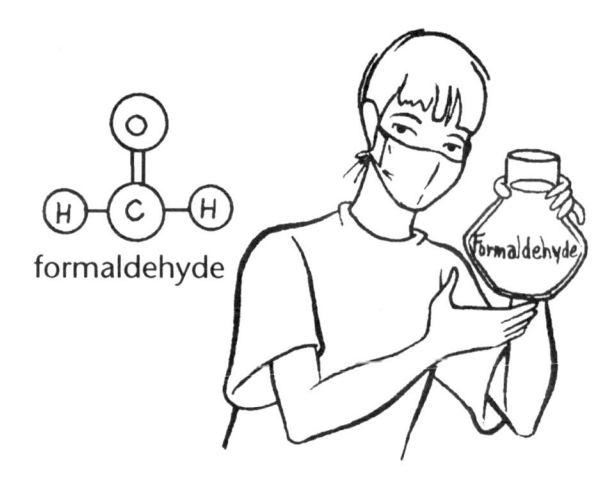

Step 1: Formaldehyde has ___ atom of carbon.
Each carbon weighs ____.
___ x ___ = ___   _____

Step 2: It also has ___ atoms of hydrogen.
Each hydrogen weighs ____.
___ x ___ = ___   _____

Step 3: Last, formaldehyde has ___ atom of oxygen. Each oxygen weighs ____.
___ x ___ = ___   _____

Total: _____

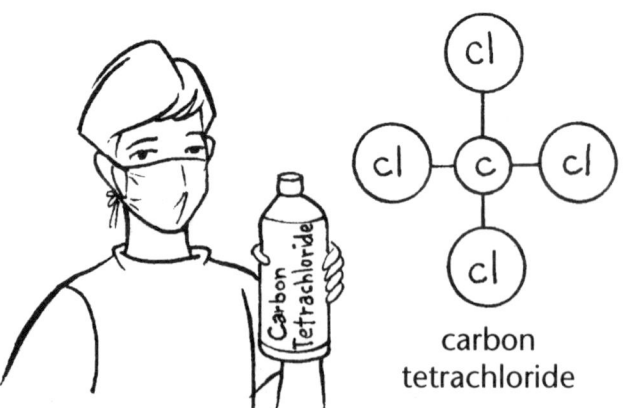

formaldehyde

Step 1: Carbon tetrachloride has ___ atom of carbon. The carbon weighs ____.
___ x ___ = ___   _____

Step 2: It also has ___ atoms of chlorine.
Each chlorine weighs ____.
___ x ___ = ___   _____

Total: _____

carbon tetrachloride

What's the Matter?

So, WHAT *IS* THE MATTER? All matter could be found as three different forms: **solid**, **liquid**, or **gas**.

Glass, paper, and ice are examples of solids. Solids have a shape that's fixed (that is, the shape doesn't change). Solids have a fixed **volume**, too (volume is the space that matter takes up). Solids are *solid* because the molecules in them are packed very closely together. They can't move very much, if at all. Another way of understanding solids is that the molecules in them have very little energy.

HERE ARE SOME EXAMPLES OF SOLIDS.

I WONDER HOW DO MOLECULES PACK CLOSE TOGETHER TO GIVE SOLIDS THEIR SHAPES?

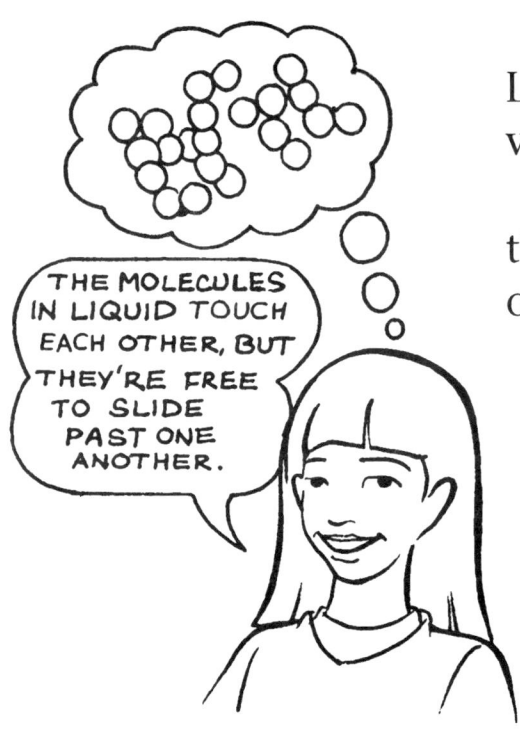

THE MOLECULES IN LIQUID TOUCH EACH OTHER, BUT THEY'RE FREE TO SLIDE PAST ONE ANOTHER.

Milk, oil, and shampoo are all liquids. Liquids can change their shape, but not their volume.

The molecules in a liquid have more energy than those in a solid. Thus, they can move over and around each other. They can move farther away from each other than the molecules in a solid, but they can't actually separate. For that, the liquid molecules would need more energy.

Gases have that energy. Helium, oxygen, and carbon dioxide are examples of gases. Gases can take any shape they like. They

Do You Know Your Solids, Liquids, and Gases?
The boxes on the right each describe a solid, liquid, or gas.
Match each word below to the correct box.

liquid •

⇨ The molecules in this are tightly packed.
⇨ The molecules don't have the energy to move around much.
⇨ This can't change its shape or volume.

⇨ The molecules in this are loosely packed.
⇨ The molecules have the energy to move around a lot, but they can't separate from each other.
⇨ This can change its shape but not its volume.

gas •

solid •

⇨ The molecules in this aren't packed at all.
⇨ The molecules have lots of energy and move all over the place.
⇨ This can change its shape and its volume.

can be squeezed into small spaces or spread out into large spaces. They can do that because the molecules in gases have the energy needed to bounce all around and not stay close together.

THE MOLECULES IN GAS FLOAT AROUND FREELY.

gas   liquid   solid

Any **substance** (matter) can come in all three forms: gas, liquid, or solid. It just depends on how much energy the molecules in the substance have.

⇨ ⇨ ⇨ Go to page 53!

What Kind of Matter Is It?

In the pictures below, you'll see some solids, liquids, and gases. Can you tell which is which? In the blank line next to each of the items listed below, write **S** for solid, **L** for liquid, or **G** for gas.

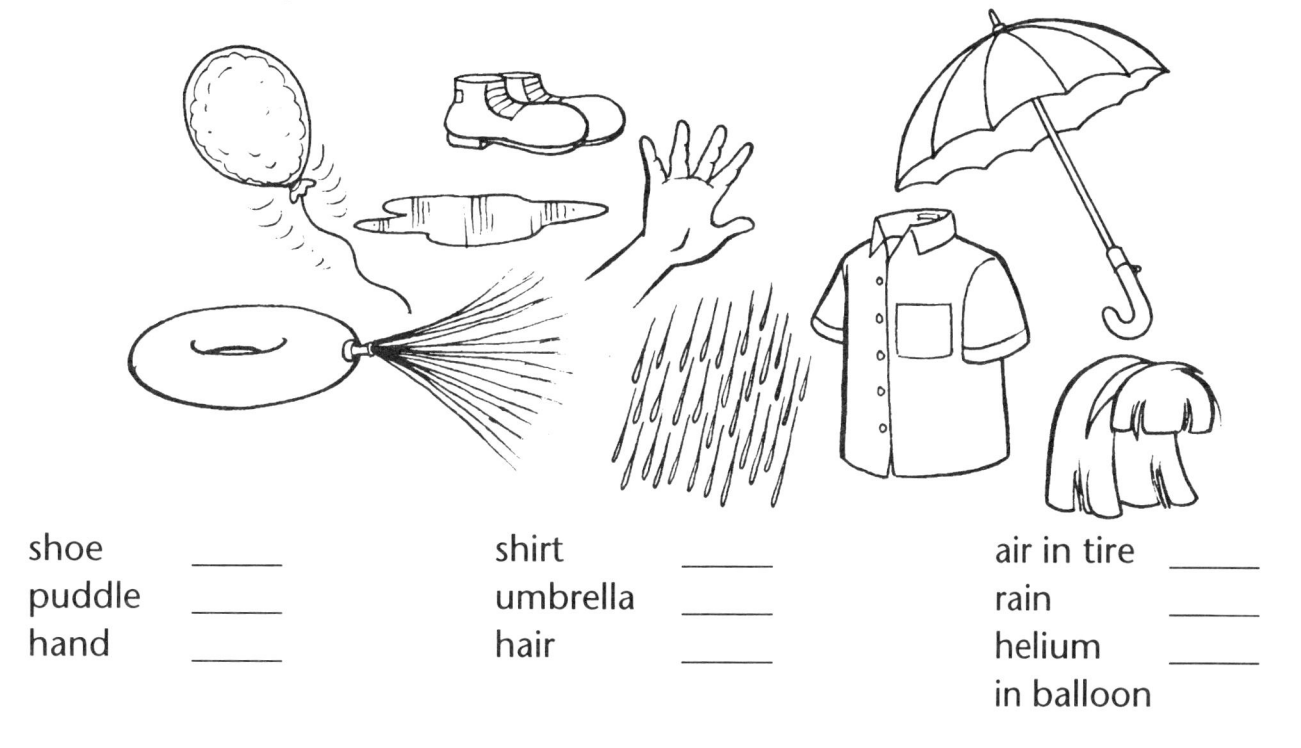

shoe _____	shirt _____	air in tire _____
puddle _____	umbrella _____	rain _____
hand _____	hair _____	helium _____
		in balloon

Which Weighs the Most?

Take a guess: Is a box of liquid lighter than a box of gas? Is it heavier, maybe? How would you put a solid, liquid, and gas in order by weight? Using words from the Word Box, fill in the blanks to find out the answers to these questions.

Imagine a ___(2)___. Think about how much ___(12)___ or ___(6)___ or ___(4)___ you could ___(13)___ into the ___(2)___. ___(1)___ the ___(8)___ in a ___(12)___ are ___(10)___ together ___(14)___, you could ___(13)___ ___(9)___ ___(12)___ into the ___(2)___ than a ___(6)___. ___(1)___ the ___(8)___ in a ___(6)___ are ___(10)___ ___(9)___ ___(3)___ together than in a ___(4)___, you could ___(13)___ ___(9)___ ___(6)___ into the ___(2)___ than gas.

Word Box
1 Because
2 box
3 closely
4 gas
5 heavier
6 liquid
7 mean
8 molecules
9 more
10 packed
11 rule
12 solid
13 stuff
14 tightly
15 water

What does all this ___(7)___? A ___(12)___ is ___(5)___ than a ___(6)___, and a ___(6)___ is ___(5)___ than a ___(4)___. This is the ___(11)___, except for one of the most important molecules of life: ___(15)___. ___(1)___ ___(12)___ ice is less ___(10)___ than ___(6)___ ___(15)___, ice is lighter than ___(15)___. That's why ice floats in ___(15)___.

52

Speaking of gases, liquids and solids, let's take water as an example.

If enough energy is taken away from steam, it turns into liquid water. If even more energy is taken away, the water turns into solid ice!

In this book, you have learned a lot about matter—including atoms and molecules, ions and isotopes, and solids, liquids, and gases. Are you ready to test what you know? On the next page, you'll see some definitions. Each one goes with a word from the Word Box. If you do a good job matching them up, a certificate is waiting for you at the end of the book!

CHECK OUT THE SCIENCE WORDS!

Do you remember reading about each of the words below? When you think you know the meaning of a word, put a ✓ in the box next to it.

- ❏ volume
- ❏ solid
- ❏ liquid
- ❏ gas
- ❏ substance

The Final Match-Up

Here's what to do: Each of the words in the Word Box has a definition it belongs with. Match up the words and definitions by filling in the blanks with the correct words.

1. _____: An atom that has either a positive or negative charge because it has lost or gained one or more electrons.

2. _____: An atom that has a different number of neutrons than the number of protons or electrons it has.

3. _____: The number of protons in an atom's nucleus.

4. _____: A property of matter that has to do with electric and magnetic forces. There are two forms: positive and negative.

5. _____: Another word for "stuff."

6. _____: Atoms connected together to make a new substance. Water is an example.

7. _____: Different types of atoms. Each type has a different number of protons in its nucleus.

Word Box
- atomic number
- charge
- ion
- isotope
- matter
- molecule
- elements

Answer Sheet

Page 6
idea

Page 7
1-10: Nice try
11-15: Good job
16-20: Very nice job
21-30: Excellent
More than 30: Fantastic

Page 8

(word search grid with circled words: PARTICLE, ATOM, WOOD, etc.)

Page 9
TWO KINDS OF FORCES PLAY IMPORTANT ROLES IN ATOMS.

Page 10
THEY ARE ELECTRIC AND NUCLEAR FORCES.

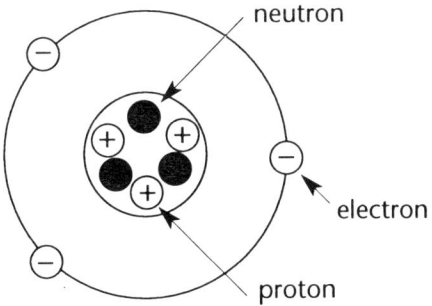

Page 11
3 electorns
3 neutrons
3 protons

(diagram of atom with neutron, electron, proton labeled)

Electrons are located at the outer part of an atom.

Page 12

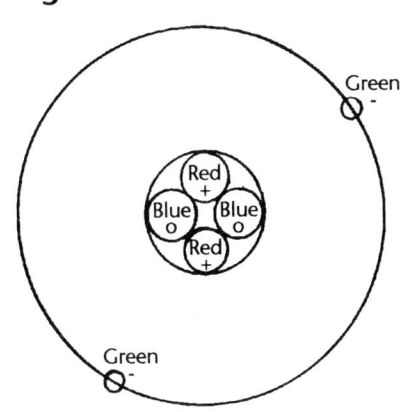

(diagram of atom with Red protons, Blue neutrons, and Green electrons)

Page 16

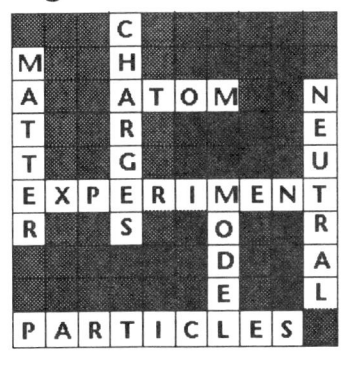

(crossword with answers: MATTER, CHARGES, ATOM, NEUTRAL, EXPERIMENT, MODE, PARTICLES)

Page 17
A hydrogen atom
A carbon atom
An oxygen atom

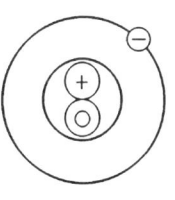

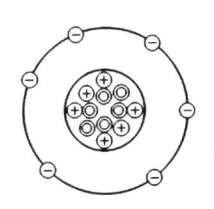

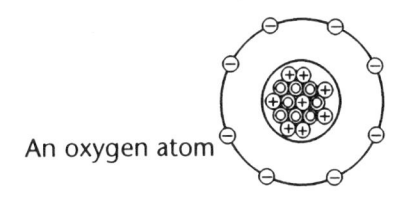

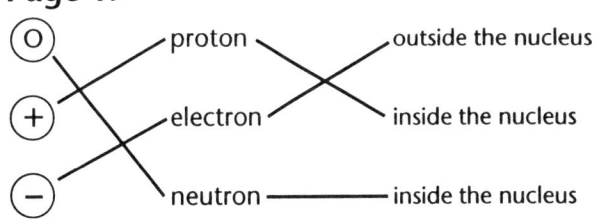

Page 19
○ —— proton —— outside the nucleus
⊕ —— electron —— inside the nucleus
⊖ —— neutron —— inside the nucleus

Page 20

element	symbol	weight	order by weight
oxygen	O	16	2
carbon	C	12	1
uranium	U	238	5
aluminum	Al	27	3
sulfur	S	32	4

Answer Sheet

Page 21
mato	atom	ooptise	isotope
cleeontr	electron*	garceh	charge
oin	ion	norpto	proton*
esstnciti	scientist	trapelic	particle*

Page 23
neutral
positive
negative
neutral
negative

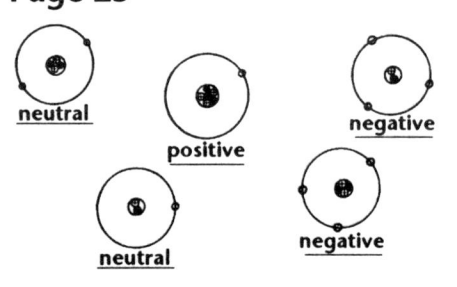

Page 27
N 7 14 Nitrogen
O 8 16 Oxygen
C 6 12 Carbon
H 1 1 Hydrogen

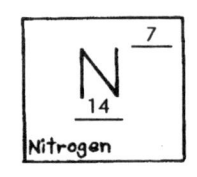

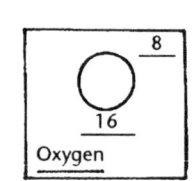

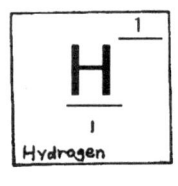

Page 29

Element Name	Atomic Symbol	Atomic Number	Atomic Weight
Fluorine	F	9	19
Potassium	K	19	39
Titanium	Ti	22	48
Iron	Fe	26	56
Nickel	Ni	28	59
Krypton	Kr	36	84
Lead	Pb	82	207
Uranium	U	92	238
Californium	Cf	98	251
Einsteinium	Es	99	254
Mendelevium	Md	101	258

1. Flourine has 9 protons.
   Krypton has 36 protons.
2. Mandelevium
3. Yes

Page 30
A is hydrogen
B is carbon

Page 31
C is oxygen
D is lithium
E is nitrogen

Page 33
iodine B4
silver A2
copper B2
hydrogen B1
oxygen A1
diamond A3
mercury B3

Page 34
Inside me are electrons, neutrons, and protons. I am the smallest piece of stuff possible.
What am I? **atom**

I am a kind of atom. I can be gold, oxygen, sodium, tin, copper, nitrogen, neon, or many other things. In fact, there are 109 different kinds of me.
What am I? **element**

I can be an atom or molecule. I can be a rock, star, ice cube, jacket, bug, book, or anything else. I take up space and weigh something.
What am I? **matter**

I am a kind of atom. I might have too many electrons or not enough. I am not neutral but charged.
What am I? **ion**

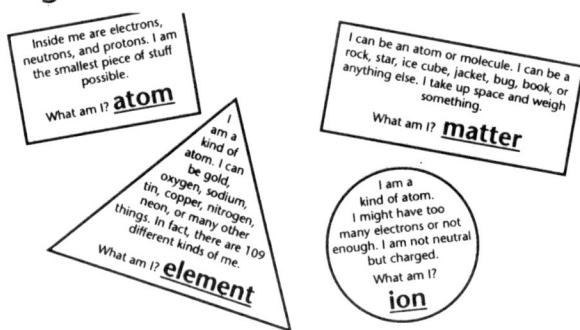

Page 37
Lithium
Boron
Neon
Nitrogen

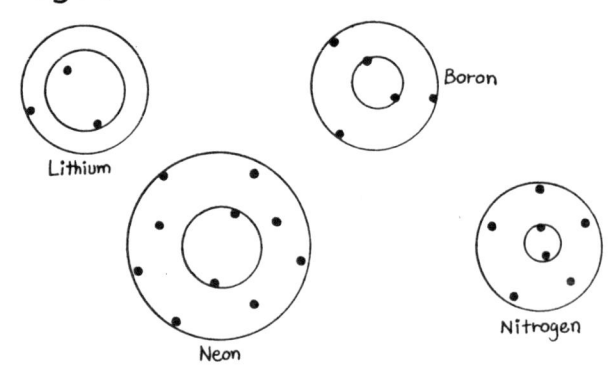

Page 38
ELECTORNS MAKE EACH ELEMENT UNIQUE. ELECTRONS RULE!

Page 39
Neon and Argon
Boron and Aluminum

56

Answer Sheet

Page 40

An atom is most stable ("happy") when it has 8 electrons in its outer shells and 2 electrons in its most inner shell. Oxygen has 6 electrons in its outer shell so it needs to gain 2 more to be stable ("happy").

Lithium has one electron in its outer shell. It would be more stable if it lost that one electron from its outer shell and just have the 2 electrons in its most inner shell.

Beryilium would be more stable if it looses its 2 electrons in its outer shell.

Page 42

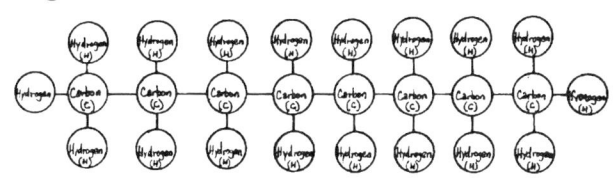

8 carbon atoms
18 hydrogen atoms
25 bonds

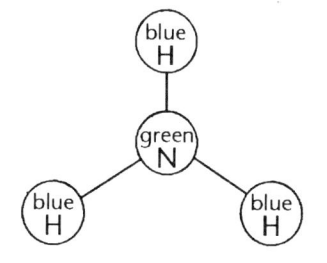

Page 43

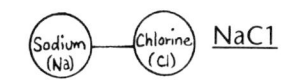

NaCl

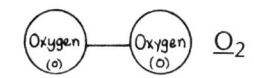

O_2

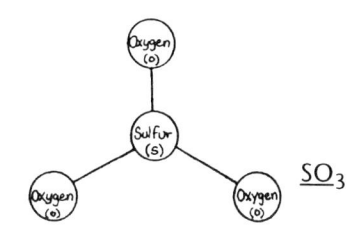

SO_3

Page 45
Molecular weight of NaCl is 58

Page 45

1. atoms
2. sciences
3. isotopes
4. elemental
5. ionic
6. molecules
7. elements
8. atomic
9. ions
10. scientific
11. nuclear
12. scientist
13. molecular

Page 47

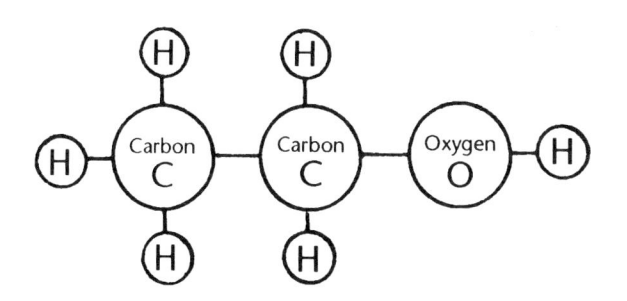

Step 1: Ethanol has **2** atoms of carbon.
   Each carbon weighs **12**.
   2 x **12** = **24** **24**

Step 2: It also has 6 atoms of hydrogen.
   Each hydrogen weighs **1**.
   6 x **1** = **6**......................**6**

Step 3: Finally, it has **1** atom of oxygen.
   Each oxygen weighs **16**.
   1 x **16** = **16** **16**

Total: **46**

Answer Sheet

Page 48

Step 1: Acetone has **3** atoms of carbon.
Each carbon weighs **12**
3 x **12** = **36**   36

Step 2: It also has **6** atoms of hydrogen.
Each hydrogen weighs **1**
6 x **1** = **6**   6

Step 3: Last, acetone has **1** atom of oxygen.
Each oxygen weighs **16**
1 x **16** = **16**   16

Total: 58

Step 1: Formaldehyde has **1** atom of carbon.
Each carbon weighs **12**
1 x **12** = **12**   12

Step 2: It also has **2** atoms of hydrogen.
Each hydrogen weighs **1**
2 x **1** = **2**   2

Step 3: Last, formaldehyde has **1** atom of oxygen. Each oxygen weighs **16**
1 x **16** = **16**   16

Total: 30

Step 1: Carbon tetrachloride has **1** atom of carbon. The carbon weighs **12**
1 x **12** = **12**   12

Step 2: It also has **4** atoms of chlorine.
Each chlorine weighs **35**
4 x **35** = **140**   140

Total: 152

Page 50

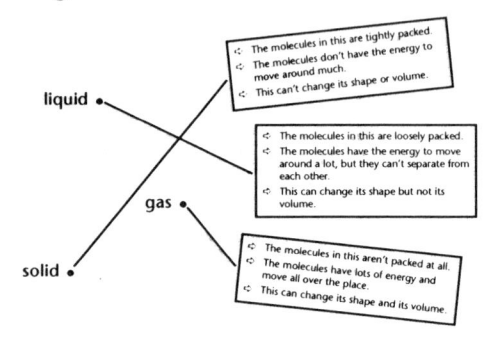

liquid → The molecules in this are loosely packed. The molecules have the energy to move around a lot, but they can't separate from each other. This can change its shape but not its volume.

gas → The molecules in this aren't packed at all. The molecules have lots of energy and move all over the place. This can change its shape and its volume.

solid → The molecules in this are tightly packed. The molecules don't have the energy to move around much. This can't change its shape or volume.

Page 51

shoe **S**   shirt **S**   air in tire **G**
puddle **L**   umbrella **S**   rain **L**
hand **S**   hair **S**   helium in balloon **G**

Page 52

Imagine a **box**. Think about how much **solid** or **liquid** or **gas** you could **stuff** into the **box**. Because the **molecules** in a **solid** are **packed** together **tightly**, you could **stuff** **more** **stuff** into the **box** than a **liquid**. Because the **molecules** in a **liquid** are **packed** **more** **closely** together than in a **gas**, you could **stuff** **more** **liquid** into the **box** than gas.

What does all this **mean**? A **solid** is **heavier** than a **liquid**, and a **liquid** is **heavier** than a **gas**. This is the **rule**, except for one of the most important molecules of life: **water**. **Because** **solid** ice is less **packed** than **liquid** **water**, ice is lighter than **water**. That's why ice floats in **water**.

Page 54

1. ion
2. isotope
3. atomic number
4. charge
5. matter
6. molecule
7. element

58

In recognition for the successful completion of
What's the Matter?
The Story of Atoms and Molecules

_____
Name

has hereby earned the title

Science Kid!